PENGUIN BOOKS

PORCUPINES

Graham Higgin was born in Belfast in 1968. He studied history at Cambridge University and philosophy at Yale University. A writer of poetry and fiction, he also curates shows of contemporary art. He lives in London.

GRAHAM HIGGIN

Porcupines

A PHILOSOPHICAL
ANTHOLOGY

PENGUIN BOOKS

PENGUIN BOOKS

Published by the Penguin Group
Penguin Books Ltd, 27 Wrights Lane, London w8 5TZ, England
Penguin Putnam Inc., 375 Hudson Street, New York, New York 10014, USA
Penguin Books Australia Ltd, Ringwood, Victoria, Australia
Penguin Books Canada Ltd, 10 Alcorn Avenue, Toronto, Ontario, Canada M4V 3B2
Penguin Books India (P) Ltd, 11, Community Centre, Panchsheel Park, New Delhi – 110 017, India
Penguin Books (NZ) Ltd, Private Bag 102902, NSMC, Auckland, New Zealand
Penguin Books (South Africa) (Pty) Ltd, 5 Watkins Street, Denver Ext 4, Johannesburg 2094, South Africa

Penguin Books Ltd, Registered Offices: Harmondsworth, Middlesex, England

First published by Allen Lane The Penguin Press 1999
Published in Penguin Books 2000
1

Copyright © Graham Higgin, 1999
All rights reserved

The moral right of the author has been asserted

Printed in England by Clays Ltd, St Ives plc

Contents

[v

Acknowledgements

The author and publishers would like to express their gratitude to [**vii**
the following organizations and individuals for granting permission
to cite their copyright material.

Athlone Press: *Positions* by Jacques Derrida, translated by Alan Bass
(1982); Professor Lewis White Beck: *The Critique of Practical Reason* by
Immanuel Kant, translated by Lewis White Beck (University of
Chicago Press, 1949); Blackwell Publishers: *The Philosophical
Investigations* by Ludwig Wittgenstein, translated by G. E. Anscombe,
(1968); *Culture and Value* by Ludwig Wittgenstein, translated by G. H.
Von Wright (1980); Cambridge University Press: *The Presocratic
Philosophers*, edited and translated by G. S. Kirk, J. E. Raven and M.
Schofield (1983); *The Hellenistic Philosophers, Texts and Translations*,
edited and translated by A. A. Long and D. N. Sedley (2 vols.,
1987); *The Outlines of Scepticism* by Sextus Empiricus, translated by
Julia Annas and Jonathan Barnes (1994); *Machine Man and other
Writings* by Julien Offray de La Mettrie, edited and translated by
Ann Thompson (1996); *Reason, Truth and History* by Hilary Putnam
(1981); *Realism and Reason: Philosophical Papers Vol. 3* by Hilary Putnam
(1983); Jonathan Cape: *Aphorisms* by Georg Christophe Lichtenberg,
translated by Franz Mautner and Harry Hatfield (1969); The
Continuum Publishing Company: *Negative Dialectics* by Theodor W.
Adorno, translated by E. B. Ashton (Copyright © 1973 by The
Continuum Publishing Company. Reprinted by permission of The
Continuum Publishing Company.); Cornell University Press: *The
New Science* by Giambattista Vico, translated by Thomas Goddard
Bergin and Max Harold Frisch (1984); J. M. Dent: *The Discourses and
Handbook* by Epictetus, translated by Elizabeth Carter, revised by
Robin Hard (Everyman, 1995); *The Social Contract and Discourses* by
Jean-Jacques Rousseau, translated by G. D. H. Cole (Everyman,

1913, 1968); Dover Publications Inc.: *The World as Will and Representation* by Arthur Schopenhauer, translated by E. F. J. Payne (1969); Duquesne University Press: *Totality and Infinity* by Emmanuel Levinas, translated by Alphonso Lingis (1969); Catherine Z. Elgin, literary executor of Nelson Goodman, for permission to quote from: *Problems and Projects* (Bobbs-Merrill, 1972) and *Ways of Worldmaking* (Hackett, 1978); Encyclopædia Britannica: *Rules for the Direction of the Mind and other Writings* by René Descartes, translated by E. S. Haldane and G. R. T. Ross (Great Books of the Western World, 1954); Hackett Publishing Company: *Phaedrus* by Plato, translated by Alexander Nehamas and Paul Woodruff (1995); *Hellenistic Philosophy: Introductory Readings*, edited and translated by Brad Inwood and L. P. Gerson (1988); *The Nichomachean Ethics* by Aristotle, translated by Terence Irwin (1985); *Philosophical Writings* by William of Ockham, translated by Philotheus Boehner, revised by Stephen F. Brown (1990); *Philosophical Essays* by G. W. Leibniz, edited and translated by Roger Ariew and Daniel Garber (1989); *The Critique of Judgement* by Immanuel Kant, translated by Werner S. Pluhar (1987); Harcourt Brace & Company: *Philosophy Is For Everyman* by Karl Jaspers, translated by R. F. C. Hall and Grete Wels (1968); *Illuminations* by Walter Benjamin, edited by Hannah Arendt, translated by Harry Zohn (Harcourt, Brace & World Inc., 1968); HarperCollins Publishers: *Heidegger: Basic Writings* by Martin Heidegger, edited and translated by Frank A. Capuzzi, J. Glenn Gray and David Farrell Krell (1977); *On The Way To Language* by Martin Heidegger, translated by Peter D. Hertz (1971); *Poetry, Language, Thought* by Martin Heidegger, translated by Albert Hofstadter (1971); *The Essential Writings* by John Dewey, edited David Sidorsky (1977); Harvard University Press: *From a Logical Point of View* by W. V. O. Quine (copyright © 1953, 1961, 1981, by the President and Fellows of Harvard College; reprinted by permission of Harvard University Press); *Ontological Relativity and other Essays* by W. V. O. Quine (1969); Harvester Press UK: *The Margins of Philosophy* by Jacques Derrida, translated by Alan Bass (1986); David Higham Associates: *Philosophical Dictionary* by Voltaire, translated by Theodore Besterman (Penguin Classics, 1971); The Johns Hopkins

University Press: *Of Grammatotology* by Jacques Derrida, translated by
Gayatri Spivak (1976); Journal of Philosophy: 'Reflections on
Goodman's *Ways of Worldmaking*' by Hilary Putnam (Journal of
Philosophy, 1979, pp. 603–18); Kluwer Academic Publishers:
Cartesian Meditations by Edmund Husserl, translated by Dorion
Cairns (1991); Macmillan Press Ltd: *The Critique of Pure Reason* by
Immanuel Kant, translated by Norman Kemp Smith (Macmillan &
Co., 1929); *On History* by Immanuel Kant, edited and translated by
Lewis White Beck (Macmillan Publishing Co., 1963; *Perpetual Peace*
copyright © 1957, The Bobbs-Merrill Publishing Company); Melitta
Mew for the Estate of Sir Karl Popper: *The Myth of the Framework*
edited by M. A. Notturno (Routledge, 1994); *The Open Society and Its
Enemies* (Routledge, 2 vols., 1962); University of Minnesota Press:
Lucinde and the Fragments by Friedrich von Schlegel, edited and
translated by Peter Firchow (1971); *Visions of Excess 1927–1939* by
Georges Bataille, edited and translated by Allan Stoekl (1985);
W. W. Norton & Co.: *The Praise of Folly and Other Writings: A Norton
Critical Edition* by Desiderius Erasmus, translated by Robert M.
Adams (translation copyright © 1989 by W. W. Norton & Co., Inc.;
reprinted by permission of W. W. Norton & Co. Inc.); Oxford
University Press: *The Epicurean Fragment* by Diogenes of Oenoanda,
edited and translated by C. W. Chilton (1971); *The Proslogion* by Saint
Anselm, edited and translated by M. J. Charlesworth (Clarendon,
1965); *The Phenomenology of Spirit* by Georg Hegel, translated by A. V.
Miller (1977); *The Philosophy of Right* by Georg Hegel, translated by
T. M. Knox (1942); Paulist Press: *The Contemplative Life and Other
Writings* by Philo of Alexandria, edited and translated by David
Winton (1981); *The Soul's Journey unto God and Other Writings* by Saint
Bonaventura, edited and translated by Ewart Cousins (1978);
Penguin Books: *Early Greek Philosophy*, edited and translated by
Jonathan Barnes (Penguin Classics, 1987); *Protagoras and Meno* by
Plato, translated by W. K. C. Guthrie (Penguin Classics, 1956); *The
Symposium* by Plato, translated by Walter Hamilton (Penguin
Classics, 1951); *The Last Days of Socrates* by Plato, translated by Hugh
Tredinnick (copyright © Hugh Tredinnick 1954, 1959, 1969); *The
Republic* by Plato, translated by Sir Desmond Lee (Penguin Classics,

1974); *On The Good Life* by Cicero, edited and translated by Michael Grant (Penguin Classics, 1969); *Letters From a Stoic* by Seneca, edited and translated by Robin Campbell (Penguin Classics, 1969); *The Confessions* by Saint Augustine, translated by R. S. Pine-Coffin (Penguin Classics, 1961); *The City of God* by Saint Augustine, translated by Henry Bettenson (Penguin Classics, 1984); *The Consolation of Philosophy* by Boethius, translated by V. E. Watts (Penguin Classics, 1969); *Selected Writings* by Thomas Aquinas, edited and translated by Ralph McInerny (Penguin Classics, 1998); *Selected Writings* by Meister Eckhart, edited and translated by Oliver Davies (Penguin Classics, 1994); *The Prince* by Niccolò Machiavelli, translated by George Bull (Penguin Classics, 1961); *The Complete Essays* by Michel de Montaigne, edited and translated by M. A. Screech (Penguin Classics, 1991); *Meditations and other Metaphysical Writings* by René Descartes, edited and translated by Desmond Clarke (Penguin Classics, 1998); *Maxims* by Francois de La Rochefoucauld, translated by Leonard Tancock (Penguin Classics, 1959); *Pensées* by Blaise Pascal, translated by A. J. Krailsheimer (Penguin Classics, 1966); *Jacques the Fatalist and His Master* by Denis Diderot, translated by Michael Henry (Penguin Classics, 1986); *Essays and Aphorisms* by Arthur Schopenhauer, edited and translated by R. J. Hollingdale (Penguin Classics, 1970); *Either/Or* by Søren Kjerkegaard, translated by Alaster Hannay (Penguin Classics, 1992); *The Sickness Unto Death* by Søren Kierkegaard, translated by Alaster Hannay (Penguin Classics, 1989); *The Portable Karl Marx*, edited by Eugene Kamenka (Viking Penguin, 1983); *Twilight of the Idols and The Antichrist* by Friedrich Nietzsche, translated by R. J. Hollingdale (Penguin Classics, 1983); *Thus Spake Zarathustra* by Friedrich Nietsche, translated by R. J. Hollingdale (Penguin Classics, 1969); *The History of Sexuality, Vol. 1*, by Michel Foucault, translated by Robert Hurley (1984); *Discipline and Punish* by Michel Foucault, translated by Alan Sheridan (1979); *The Foucault Reader*, edited by Paul Rabinow (1984); Princeton University Press: *The Concept of Irony*, by Søren Kierkegaard, translated by Harold Hong and Edna Hong (1992); *Eighteen Upbuilding Discourses*, by Søren Kierkegaard, edited and translated by Harold Hong and Edna Hong (1990); *The Ethics*

Introduction

Take any one of the sentences in this book. Focus on it. Shut out
for the moment the surrounding noise. Let the pattern of words
imprint itself on your mind. Don't worry about its context for now;
just respond to the sentence in its solitude. Let it infiltrate your
brain and provoke thought. You may find images flashing up to
illustrate the sentence, or arguments trooping in to defend or assault
it. You may be remembering certain experiences which seem to
touch on what the sentence says, or even be recalling having once
thought something similar yourself. There are many ways in which
thinking may embrace the sentence and be moved by it. The chain
of associations which results from your encounter is your
commentary on the sentence. This commentary is a beginning in
philosophy.

For the Christian philosophers of medieval Europe, such as
Thomas Aquinas and William of Ockham, philosophical training
began explicitly with the writing of commentaries on a set of
sentences (the *Sententiae* compiled by Magister Peter Lombard in the
twelfth century), but all work in philosophy begins *implicitly* with a
thinking upon sentences, even if the variety and number of
philosophical sentences will always thwart any dogmatic attempt to
produce a definitive set and encapsulate them in a single book. The
philosopher is the person who submits himself day in and day out to
the test of sentences. He is one who has trained himself to think
clearly about what they mean and has become adept at sifting true
ones from false ones, using criteria which he constantly revises. He
is imaginative in drawing out the logical implications of sentences
and in giving a rigorous and intelligible shape to his commentaries.
Yet, just as dancers are not the only people who dance, so
philosophers have no monopoly over philosophizing. What your
thought traces around the sentence are perhaps your first, hesitant,

steps in philosophy. However, with practice and intellectual effort, they will be succeeded by movements becoming increasingly fluid, expansive and precise. You will be rewarded by finding that philosophical sentences which seemed to stand aloof from one another are connected in many surprising ways. They will each become a part of the commentaries which you write on the others, and, as they shake off their isolation, philosophy itself will begin to come together for you as an elaborate and ongoing commentary on life.

The procedure involved in selecting the sentences in this anthology might be compared to the ways in which fossil-hunters or beachcombers go about their pursuits. The anthology would then be like the showcase which displays the fossils chipped out of the rock or the shells gleaned from the sand. However, fossil-hunting and beachcombing irrevocably change the environments they touch. They remove the objects which please them and take possession of them; the environment is lessened as the collection expands. Garnering sentences, on the other hand, being a work of the mind, is more ecologically sound than the other two. While it does extract sentences, at one and the same time it leaves them in place. On this book's right-hand pages a sentence appears severed from its matrix, while on the left-hand page it is shown still in place, its context intact. For this reason, anthologizing would be more justly compared to the activity which you are engaged in at this very moment. Reading passes through a text, extracting sentences one by one, then returns them to the identical place in which they were found, leaving no trace of its intervention. Leaving *no* trace? Perhaps it would be better to say that reading leaves a barely perceptible scar on the texts it ghosts through. When a sentence has really grabbed you, when a sentence has leaped out at you and made you think, it can never be flawlessly reinserted into the text. After the book is closed, it continues to radiate like an ember among ashes, and whenever you think of the text you will recall that sentence raised up from the others and burnished. This anthology gathers the sentences which quietly gleam in the books which an individual reading has closed behind it. It has been able to do this because sentences are among those entities, like numbers and superhuman mothers, which have the magical ability to be always in two places at once.

To the extent that the sentences are set apart and mounted for inspection against the white of the page, they do share with those fossils and shells gathered into collections the privilege of being *specimens*. The sentences want to be taken as representative samples of the works of which they are a part. In particular, most of the chosen sentences hope to illustrate a dominant philosophical theme in their author's work or in the broader stratum of questioning and answering characteristic of the period to which his birth has assigned him. Thus the four sentences selected from Plato's dialogues deal with four major themes of his thought: how philosophy brings the soul to a recognition of its own immortality; how doing good requires knowing what goodness is; how only philosophy can transcend the error of the senses and lead the mind to true knowledge; how divinely inspired madness has a privileged access to beauty. Each of these sentences also, it is hoped, captures something of the figurative ebullience of Plato's style. Although the majority of the sentences serve a similar function in the economy of the book to the one that Plato's serve, there are a few scattered sentences which have been included because of the way they reflect back on the nature of philosophical sentences themselves. Sentences from Bruno, Vico, Schlegel and Wittgenstein are of this sort. They are like mirrors suspended behind the other sentences in order to reveal a previously hidden depth.

Now, an incisive objection may be raised to *Porcupines* at this point. The sentences, it may say, flatter to deceive. Their claim to be representatives of their discourses is a mere vanity. They can no more illustrate philosophical themes than $E = mc^2$ emblazoned on a T-shirt can give you an insight into Einstein's theory of special relativity. These sentences put up on display are specious and superficial things, the objection runs. They may give you the 'touch and feel' of philosophical writing, but can never introduce you to the chaste pleasures of philosophical mastery. That requires years of study. What is missing from these sentences, the objection may conclude, is philosophy itself.

To this objection I concede almost everything. The sentences are *merely* specimens. They are starting points for commentaries, stimuli for the reader's own investigations. That is why they are presented not just alone but also in their context, and are accompanied by related passages from the work of the same philosopher or kindred philosophers. As the reader thinks about the sentences, it is hoped that he or she will be lured back towards their native habitats following the signposts the anthology provides. There a truer understanding of their philosophical significance can be gained by thinking about the sentences which frame them and which they in turn frame. The sentences, therefore, can be imagined as wildlife postcards or exotic animal pin-ups sent back from a voyage around the philosophical archipelago, and on the back of all of them you can take as written, 'Wish you were here!'

The style of philosophical sentences gravitates towards either one of two poles – sinuous prolixity on the one hand, terse concision on the other. The latter type is best exemplified by those short, sharp sentences called maxims, aphorisms or epigrams. The former type perhaps reaches an apogee of complexity (and difficulty) in Hegel's *Phenomenology of Spirit*. There are specimens of both sorts of sentence in this anthology, although aphorisms are very much in the majority – because often the most trenchant thoughts of philosophers travel in the most streamlined vehicles.

According to Plato, the aphorism was the most ancient form of philosophical style. Enamoured with the laconic speech of the Spartans, the old sages of Greece pared their philosophical language to the bone. It was as if they wanted to fashion arrows out of language, the better to lodge knowledge in the memories of their listeners. The sentences were sharpened to a point and launched against the monsters of barbarism and ignorance. Hence it was vital that this fletcher-art of maxim-making was constantly developing more piercing forms. Democritus, the inventor of the first atomic theory of matter, devised maxims which were quick shafts of wisdom. Their basic design is admirable. 'In fleeing death, men pursue it.' 'Fools, fearing death, desire life.' An antithesis is set up across a central caesura (fleeing/pursuing; fearing/desiring). The two sides of the statement are like the two arms of a balance given the same initial weight. There is a kind of rhythmic symmetry or metrical equilibrium at work in the structure. However, as reading-hearing sweeps consciousness over the fulcrum, the balance tilts and the penny drops. Insight is delivered as irrevocably as a judgement of the scales. It has, for good reason, proved a long-lived model, and is found, with measured variations, in sentences chosen from La Rochefoucauld, Pascal, Voltaire, Rousseau, Kant, Lichtenberg, Schlegel, Nietzsche and Wittgenstein. Aphorisms are the well-honed thoughts and tempered weapons of philosophers. Like Montaigne, who avidly tracked aphorisms down in his reading and inscribed his favourites on the ceiling of his study, this anthology has sought out some of the most formidable and hung them like trophies on the walls of the book.

With the late Latin texts of philosophers such as Erasmus and Bruno a marked inflation in average sentence length seems to occur. This increase subsequently becomes an explosion of growth in the Early Modern vernacular texts of Bacon, Descartes and Hobbes, until one finds oneself enmeshed in the arabesque mazes of Locke and Berkeley, through which *ideas* pursue one another in a breathless game of tag. There seems to be an unspoken principle at work in such writings – namely, to get as much value as possible out of each sentence, as if it were a tract of land to be cultivated and fertility was synonymous with prolixity. While aphorisms manage to seem as archaic as oracular pronouncements and as modern as advertising slogans, the sentences of Locke and Berkeley often bespeak a period and style which is now distinctly old-fashioned. These philosophers' works are monuments to the semicolon, a punctuation mark contemporary society seems bent on abolishing along with other relics of that aristocratic and ecclesiastical past when a more easeful use of time held sway. However, it would be a mistake to confuse the styles of Locke and Berkeley with the rambling verbosity of clubbable bores. On the contrary, their sentences delight in the most playful use of literary figures, in particular the elaborately extended metaphor. They are never guilty of the legalistic contortionism which Bentham might have served time for had violence against language been an indictable offence. Rather, they are highly deft conceptual jugglers, masters of the art of keeping as many *ideas* in circulation as possible without allowing the sub-clauses to collapse in a heap or the main metaphor to collide jarringly with the sub-metaphors. Schopenhauer and Mill are also both talented gravity-defiers of this sort, but perhaps the best example of this art is not in their work or in Locke's or Berkeley's, but is Nietzsche's pulsating evocation of the world as a sea of forces, flowing and rushing, wave upon wave (see page 167). In this passage, language becomes infused with the fervour of a thinking which is not satisfied with merely representing its image of the world but seeks to translate the internal forces which restlessly animate it, and which a formal description could capture only as inert quantities, into rhythms which can with justice be called musical. The text breathes and sings. Wittgenstein's demand for philosophy to be written as poetic composition is here fulfilled. Nietzsche's writing, composed as it is of the most acute aphoristic shards and the most compelling oceanic sentences, must stand as an exemplar of philosophical style at its richest and most vibrant. You will find expressions of both extremes entered in black in the pages that follow.

In exploring the archive of Western philosophy one is amazed at the intricacy of the edifice which the philosophers have built. This anthology represents merely a short journey through that library of theirs, which is inexhaustible not only because it, like our universe, is constantly expanding, but also because there exists an indefinite number of potential connections between the sentences which have already been stored. Yet this journey, whistle-stop as it is, has amassed a substantial debt to the philosophers and scholars who have pieced together a labyrinth of reason from the debris of Babel. For, in its twists and turns, elegant staircases, trapdoors, blind alleys, vicious circles and false exits, thought is moving through a model which mirrors its own perplexity in the face of the world. In complications and through perplexity thought thrives, and even if the labyrinth must always pose more questions than it resolves and only ever opens on to further reaches of itself, the thinking traveller, as long as he or she keeps in motion, will always have the jump on the Minotaur (that hybrid of stupidity, melancholy and boredom) who lurks where death's shadow falls, greedy to gobble up life and thought. Mazement, amazing as it may seem, protects. The custodians of one entrance to the labyrinth, the librarians of the British Library in London, have my sincere gratitude for so amiably helping me to delve (Sita Gunasingham especially), and my commissioning editor, Stefan McGrath, also has my heartfelt thanks for tugging now and again at the deadline end of the thread.

A fragment, like a miniature work of art, has to be entirely isolated from the surrounding world and be complete in itself like a porcupine. FRIEDRICH VON SCHLEGEL

The maxim is closed because it is armed.

ROLAND BARTHES

In the first book of my *Epigrams* or *Poems in All Metres* there is an epigram on Thales:

When once he was watching a gymnastic
      contest, O Zeus of the Sun,
you stole Thales the Sage from the stadium.
I praise you for bringing him near to you; for
      the old man
could no longer see the stars from the earth.

The motto '**Know Thyself**' is his, though Antisthenes in his *Successions* says that it was Phemonoe's and that Chilon appropriated it.

Diogenes Laertius, *Lives of the Philosophers*, 1.40[1]

There are some, both in the present day and in the past, who have understood that to be Spartan implies a taste for intellectual rather than physical exercise, for they have realized that the art of framing brief, taut and telling phrases is a mark of the highest culture. Of these were Thales of Miletus, Pittacus of Mytilene, Bias of Priene, our own Solon, Cleobolus of Lindus and Myson of Chen, and the seventh of their company, we are told, was a Spartan, Chilon. All these were emulators, admirers and disciples of Spartan culture, and their wisdom was of the Spartan type, consisting of pithy and memorable dicta uttered by each. Moreover, they met together and dedicated the first fruits of their wisdom to Apollo in his temple at Delphi, inscribing those words which are on everyone's lips, '**Know Thyself**' and 'Nothing in excess'. I mention these facts to stress that among the ancients, this Laconic brevity was the characteristic form of philosophy.

Plato, *Protagoras*, 342e–343b[2]

2]

Know Thyself.

Xenophanes, teaching that God is one and incorporeal, is therefore correct in saying:

There is one God, greatest among gods and men, similar to mortals in neither form nor thought.

And again:

Men have the notion that gods are born and wear clothes and have voice and shape.

And again:

But if cattle and horses or lions had hands, or were able to draw with their hands and do the works that men can do, horses would draw the form of their gods like horses, and cattle like cattle, and they would make their gods' bodies resemble their own.

Clement of Alexandria, *Miscellanies*, s.109[1]

But if cattle and horses or lions had hands, or were able to draw with their hands and do the works that men can do, horses would draw the form of their gods like horses, and cattle like cattle, and they would make their gods' bodies resemble their own.

. . . the ancients hint at a sort of divine
war, for Heraclitus speaks as follows:
**Know then that war is common,
that justice is strife, and that all
things come to be in accordance
with strife and necessity.**

Origen, *Against Celsus*, 6.42[1]

6] 'Listening not to me but to the *Logos*,'
says Heraclitus, 'it is wise to agree that
all things are one.' And because all men
do not acknowledge this, he reproves
them in the following way: 'They do not
understand how something can be
wrenched away from itself and yet at the
same time be brought into balance like
the counter-stretched poise of the bow
and the lyre.' . . . That the universe is a
child and an eternal king of everything,
he says in the following way: 'Eternity is
a child at play, shunting draught-pieces:
the kingdom is in a child's hands.' That
the father of everything that has come
about is both begotten and unbegotten,
creature and creator, we hear in the
phrase: 'War is father of all, king of all:
some it shows as gods, some as men,
some it makes slaves, some free.'

Hippolytus, *Refutation of All Heresies*, 9.9[2]

Know then that war is common,
that justice is strife, and that all
things come to be in accordance
with strife and necessity.

That there is one and the same account
[*logos*] of everything, the account of what
is, Parmenides states in the following
words:

**Whatever is for being and for thinking
must be; for it can be, and nothing can
not.**

8]   Now if whatever anyone says or thinks is
being, then there will be one account of
everything, the account of what is.

   Simplicius, *Commentary on the Physics*, 86.25–
   30[1]

STRANGER: The audacity of the
statement lies in its implication that
'what is not' has being, for in no other
way could a falsehood come to have
being. But, my young friend, when we
were of your age the great Parmenides
from beginning to end testified against
this, constantly telling us what he also
says in his poem, 'Never shall this be
proved – that things that are not are,
but do thou, in thy inquiry, hold back
thy thought from this way.'

   Plato, *Sophis*, 237a[2]

Parmenides writes:
The same thing are thinking and a thought
   that it is.
For without what is, in which it has been
   expressed,
you will not find thinking. For nothing either
   is or will be
other than what is, since fate has fettered it
to be whole and unmoving.

   Simplicius, *Commentary on the Physics*, 146.6–
   146.11[3]

Whatever is for being and for thinking must be; for it can be, and nothing can not.

Diotimus said that [Democritus]
supposed three standards: for the
apprehension of what is unclear the
standard is the apparent; for

**Appearances are a glimpse of the
obscure**

as Anaxagoras says – and Democritus
praised him for this.

10]

Sextus Empiricus, *Against the Mathematicians*,
7.90[1]

The distinguished natural scientist
Anaxagoras, attacking the senses for
their weakness, says:

We are not capable of discerning the truth by
reason of their feebleness

and he offers as a proof of their
untrustworthiness the gradual change of
colours. For if we take two colours,
black and white, and then pour from
one to the other drop by drop, our sight
will not be able to discriminate the
gradual changes even though they exist
in nature.

Ibid.[2]

On Mind [*Nous*] Anaxagoras has written
as follows:

All other things have a portion of everything
in them but Mind is infinite and self-governed
and is mixed with nothing but is all alone by
itself. For if it was not by itself, but was mixed
with anything else, it would have a share of all
things if it were mixed with any . . . and the
things that were mingled with it would hinder
it so that it could control nothing in the way it
actually does alone by itself. For it is the finest
of all things and the purest, it has all
knowledge about everything and the greatest
power; and the Mind controls all things, both
great and small, which have soul and life.

Simplicius, *Commentary on the Physics*, 164.24[3]

Appearances are a glimpse of the obscure.

**Fools – they have no far-ranging
thoughts:
they suppose that what did not exist
before comes into being
or that something may die and perish
entirely.**

These are verses of one who shouts
aloud to all who have ears that he is not
doing away with coming into being but
only with coming into being from what
does not exist, nor with destruction but
only with complete destruction, i.e.
destruction into what does not exist. If
you wish something gentler than that
savagely simple denunciation, the
following passage may even lead you to
accuse him of excessive kindness. There
Empedocles says:

No wise man in these things would suppose in
  his mind
that while men live – what they *call* life –
for so long do they exist and experience ill and
  good,
but that before they were made men, and after
  they are dissolved they are nothing.

Those are the words not of one who
denies that those who have been born
and are living exist, but rather of one
who thinks that both those who have
not yet been born and those who have
already died exist.

Plutarch, *Against Colotes*, 1113CD[1]

When Empedocles at the beginning of
his philosophy says by way of preface
that:

This ancient decree of Fate stands immortal
that if a long-lived demigod defiles
his hands with vile crimes, he will fall
from bliss into ten thousand years of exile.
Such is the way my course has been bent,
to live a fugitive from the gods and a vagrant

he's not pointing at himself alone. In
what he says about himself he shows the
condition of us all. We are pilgrims,
strangers and exiles here in the world.

Plutarch, *On Exile*, 607C[2]

Above all, [Empedocles] assents to the
idea of metempsychosis, saying:

For already I have been a boy and a girl
and a bush and a bird and a silent fish in the
  sea.

Hippolytus, *Refutation of all Heresies*, 1.3.2[3]

Fools – they have no far-ranging
    thoughts:
they suppose that what did not
    exist before comes into being
or that something may die and
    perish entirely.

The saying of Protagoras is like the views we have mentioned. He said: **'Man is the measure of all things**,' meaning simply that that which seems to exist for each man assuredly does so. If this is so, it follows that the same thing both is and is not, and is bad and good, and that the contents of all other opposite statements are true, because often some particular thing appears beautiful to some and ugly to others, and that which appears to each man is the measure.

Aristotle, *Metaphysics*, 1062b12–20[1]

THEAETETUS: Well, Socrates, it would be disgraceful for anyone, faced with the sort of encouragement you are giving, not to try his hardest to express his thoughts. So ... I think that someone *knows* something when he *perceives* it; my current opinion, at any rate, is that knowledge and perception are the same.
SOCRATES: Well done, lad! That's the way to speak up. An excellent answer! Now then, we must examine it to see if it's a mere wind egg or has some life in it. Perception, you claim, is knowledge. Yes?
THEAETETUS: Yes.
SOCRATES: The account you give of knowledge is by no means to be despised. It's what Protagoras used to say as well, though he used different words. He said, you will remember, that **'Man is the measure of all things** – both of the being of the things which are and of the non-being of the things that are not.' No doubt you have read that?
THEAETETUS: Yes, often.

Plato, *Theaetetus*, 151d–152a[2]

Man is the measure of all things.

It is worth recording Philolaus' words, for the Pythagorean says this: '**The old theologians and prophets testify that the soul has been yoked to the body as a punishment and that it is imprisoned in it as though in a tomb.**'

Clement, *Miscellanies*, 3.3.17.1[1]

There were two forms of Pythagoras' philosophy, for there were two kinds of people who practised it, the Aphorists and the Scientists. The Aphorists were admitted by the others to be Pythagoreans, but they would not admit the Scientists among his number, saying that their work derived from Hippasus, rather than Pythagoras.

The philosophy of the Aphorists consists of unproven and unargued aphorisms that one should act in such and such a way, and they attempt to preserve the other things the master said as though they were sacred dogmas.

. . . Give no advice which is not for the good of the receiver; for advice is sacred. Labour is good: pleasures of every sort are bad; for those who have been born for punishment must be punished . . . Some of the aphorisms are of this sort.

. . . The whole of their way of life is ordered with a view to following god. This is the rationale of their philosophy. For they think it absurd for men to look for the good from any source other than the gods: it is as if you were living in a monarchy and paid service to some subordinate among the citizens, ignoring the ruler of all – that, they think, is what men actually do.

Iamblichus, *On the Pythagorean Way of Life*, 81–7[2]

Some, such as the Pythagoreans and Plato, make the infinite a principle in its own right, supposing that it exists as a substance and not as an attribute of anything else. Only the Pythagoreans locate it among perceptible objects (for they do not consider that numbers are different from these) and assert that what lies outside the heavens is infinite. Plato, on the other hand, argues that nothing exists outside the heavens (the Forms are not outside, because they exist nowhere in space), yet that the infinite is present in all perceptible objects and also in the Forms.

Aristotle, *Physics*, 203a1[3]

The old theologians and prophets testify that the soul has been yoked to the body as a punishment and that it is imprisoned in it as though in a tomb.

Images are by their dress and
adornment magnificent to observe,
but they are empty of heart.

Forgetting one's own misfortunes
generates boldness.

Fools are shaped by the gifts of fortune,
those who understand such things by
the gifts of wisdom.

18] Fools, though they hate life, wish to live
from fear of Hades.

Fools live without enjoying life.

Fools desire longevity but do not enjoy
longevity.

Fools desire what is absent: what is
present, although it is more beneficial
than what is past, they squander.

In fleeing death men pursue it.

Fools give no pleasure in the whole of
their lives.

Fools, fearing death, desire life.

Many who have learned much possess
no sense.

Without intelligence, reputation and
wealth are not safe possessions.

Stobaeus, *Anthology*, 3.4.69–82[1]

According to some, Xenophanes and
Zeno of Elea and Democritus were
sceptics . . . Democritus, who does away
with qualities where he says:

By convention hot, by convention cold: in
reality atoms and void.

And again:

In reality we know nothing – for truth is in the
depths.

Diogenes Laertius, *Lives of the Philosophers*,
9.72[2]

In fleeing death men pursue it.

Never mind him, said Socrates. Now for you, my jury. I want to explain to you how it seems to me natural that a man who has really devoted his life to philosophy should be cheerful in the face of death, and confident of finding the greatest blessing in the next world when his life is finished. I will try to make it clear to you, Simmias and Cebes, how this can be so.

Ordinary people seem not to realize that those who really apply themselves in the proper way to philosophy are directly and of their own accord preparing themselves for dying and death. If this is true, and they have actually been looking forward to death all their lives, it would of course be absurd to be troubled when the event arrives for which they have so long been preparing and looking forward.

Phaedo, 63e–64a[1]

For, let me tell you, gentlemen, that to be afraid of death is only another form of thinking that one is wise when one is not: it is to think that one knows what one does not know.

Socrates' Apology, 29a[2]

There is one way, then, in which a man can be free from all anxiety about the fate of his soul – if in life he has abandoned bodily pleasures and adornments as foreign to his purpose and likely to do more harm than good and has devoted himself to the pleasures of acquiring knowledge, and so has fitted himself to await his journey to the next world by decking out his soul not in a borrowed beauty but with its own, with self-control, and goodness, and courage, and liberality, and truth.

Phaedo, 114d–e[3]

Perhaps, someone may say, 'But surely, Socrates, after you have left us you can spend the rest of your life in quietly minding your own business.'

This is the hardest thing of all to make some of you understand. If I say that this would be disobedience to God, and that is why I cannot 'mind my own business', you will not believe that I am serious. If on the other hand I tell you that to let no day pass without discussing goodness and all the other subjects about which you hear me talking and examining both myself and others is really the very best thing a man can do, and that life without this sort of examination is not worth living, you will be even less inclined to believe me. Nevertheless, that is how it is . . .

Socrates' Apology, 37e–38a[4]

For no one who is not utterly irrational and cowardly is afraid of the mere act of dying; it is evil-doing that he fears. For to arrive in the other world with a soul surcharged with many wicked deeds is the worst of all evils.

Gorgias, 522d–e[5]

Ordinary people seem not to realize that those who really apply themselves in the proper way to philosophy are directly and of their own accord preparing themselves for dying and death.

SOCRATES: But my dear Crito, why should we pay so much attention to what 'most people' think? The really reasonable people, who have more claim to be considered, will believe the facts exactly as they are.

CRITO: You can see for yourself, Socrates, that one has to think of popular opinion as well. Your present position is quite enough to show that the capacity of ordinary people for causing trouble is not confined to petty annoyances, but has hardly any limits if you once get a bad name with them.

SOCRATES: **I only wish that ordinary people *had* an unlimited capacity for doing harm, then they might have an unlimited capacity for doing good, which would be a splendid thing if it were so.** Actually they have neither. They cannot make a man wise or stupid; they simply act at random.

Crito, 44d[6]

Nor, on the other hand, do the ignorant love wisdom or desire to be wise, for the tiresome thing about ignorance is precisely this, that a man who possesses neither beauty nor goodness nor intelligence is perfectly well satisfied with himself, and no one who does not believe that he lacks a thing desires what he does not believe that he lacks.

Symposium, 204a[7]

This small company, then, when they have tasted the happiness of philosophy and seen the frenzy of the masses, understand that political life has virtually nothing sound about it, and they'll find no ally to save them in the fight for justice; and if they're not prepared to join others in their vileness and yet are unable to fight the general

barbarism single-handed, they are likely to perish like a man thrown among wild beasts, without profit to themselves or others, before they can do any good to their friends or society.

Republic, 496c–d[8]

The [ideal] society we have described can never grow into a reality or see the light of day and there will be no end to the troubles of states, or indeed, my dear Glaucon, of the human race itself, till philosophers become kings in this world, or till those we now call kings and rulers really and truly become philosophers, and political power and philosophy thus come together into the same hands, while the many natures now content to follow either to the exclusion of the other are forcibly debarred from doing so.

Ibid., 473c–d[9]

The true champion of justice, if he intends to survive even for a short time, must necessarily confine himself to private life and leave politics alone.

Socrates' Apology, 32a[10]

I only wish that ordinary people
had an unlimited capacity for
doing harm, then they might
have an unlimited power for
doing good, which would be a
splendid thing if it were so.

CEBES: What do you mean Socrates?
SOCRATES: I will explain. **Every seeker after wisdom knows that until philosophy takes it over his soul is a helpless prisoner, chained hand and foot in the body, compelled to view reality not directly but only through its prison bars, and wallowing in utter ignorance.** And philosophy can see that the imprisonment is ingeniously effected by the prisoner's own active desire, which makes him the first accessory in his own confinement. Well, philosophy takes over the soul in this condition and by gentle persuasion tries to set it free. She points out that observation by means of the eyes and ears and other senses is entirely deceptive, and she urges the soul to refrain from using them unless it is necessary to do so, and encourages it to collect and concentrate itself by itself, trusting nothing but its own independent judgement upon objects considered in themselves, and attributing no truth to anything which it views indirectly as being subject to variation, because such objects are sensible and visible but what the soul itself sees is intelligible and invisible.

Phaedo, 82d–83b[11]

Then shall we not fairly plead that our true lover of knowledge naturally strives for reality, and will not rest content with each set of particulars which opinion takes for reality, but will soar with undimmed and unwearied passion until he grasps the nature of each thing as it is in itself, with the mental faculty fitted to do so, with the faculty which is akin to reality, and which approaches and unites with it . . . and is only released

from effort when it has attained knowledge and true life and fulfilment?

Republic, 490a–b[12]

Thus the soul, since it is immortal and has been born many times, and has seen all things both here and in the other world, has learned everything there is. So we need not be surprised if it can recall the knowledge of virtue or anything else which, as we see, it once possessed. All nature is akin, and the soul has learned everything, so that when a man has recalled a single piece of knowledge – has learned it, in everyday speech – there is no reason why he should not find out all the rest, if he keeps a stout heart and does not grow weary of the search; for seeking and learning are nothing but recollection.

Meno, 81d[13]

[A] soul that never saw the truth cannot take on human shape, since a human being must understand speech in terms of general forms, proceeding to bring many perceptions together into a reasoned unity. That process is the recollection of the things our soul saw when it was travelling with god, when it disregarded the things we now call real and lifted up its head to what is truly real instead.

Phaedrus, 249b–c[14]

Every seeker after wisdom knows
that until philosophy takes it over
his soul is a helpless prisoner,
chained hand and foot in the
body, compelled to view reality
not directly but only through its
prison bars, and wallowing in
utter ignorance.

Third comes the kind of madness that is possession by the Muses, which takes a tender, virgin soul and awakens it to a Bacchic frenzy of songs and poetry that glorifies the achievements of the past and teaches them to future generations. **If anyone comes to the gates of poetry and expects to become an adequate poet by acquiring expert knowledge of the subject without the Muses' madness, he will fail, and his self-controlled verses will be eclipsed by the poetry of men who have been driven out of their minds.**

There you have some of the fine achievements – and I could tell you even more – that are due to god-sent madness.

Phaedrus, 245a[15]

AGATHON: So much then for the uprightness and self-control and courage of the god of Love; there remains his genius, and I must do my best to do justice to it. In the first place – if, like Eryximachus, I may give pride of place to my own calling – Love is himself so inspired a poet that he can make poets of others. At any rate, anyone whom Love touches becomes a poet, 'although a stranger to the Muses before'.

Symposium, 196d–e[16]

' "When a man, starting from this sensible world and making his way upward by a proper use of his feeling of love for boys, begins to catch sight of absolute beauty, he is very near his goal. This is the right way of being initiated into the mysteries of love: to begin with specimens of beauty in this world and using them as steps to ascend continually with absolute beauty as one's goal, from one instance of particular beauty to two and from two to all, then from physical beauty to ethical beauty, and from ethical beauty to the beauty of knowledge, until from knowledge of various kinds one arrives at that supreme knowledge whose sole object is absolute beauty and one gains the knowledge of what absolute beauty is.

"This above all others, my dear Socrates," Diotima continued, "is the region where a man's life should be spent, in the contemplation of absolute beauty." '

Ibid., 211c–d[17]

The mind's eye begins to see clearly when the outer eyes grow dim.

Ibid., 219a[18]

If anyone comes to the gates of
poetry and expects to become an
adequate poet by acquiring
expert knowledge of the subject
without the Muses' madness, he
will fail, and his self-controlled
verses will be eclipsed by the
poetry of men who have been
driven out of their minds.

It is also disputed whether the happy person will need friends or not. It is said that those who are blessedly happy and self-sufficient have no need of friends; for they have [all] the things that are good and hence, being self-sufficient, need nothing further, but your friend, being another self, provides what your own efforts cannot: whence the saying 'When fortune's kind, who needs friends?' However, it would seem absurd to award the happy person all good things and yet not give him friends as well, for having friends seems to be the greatest of external goods . . . **Surely it is also absurd to make the blessed person solitary; for no one would choose to possess all good things and yet remain alone, since a human being is a political creature, tending by nature to live with others.** This then will also be true of the happy person, for he has the things that are by nature good. And plainly it is better for him to spend his days with friends and good people rather than with strangers of just any character. Therefore the happy person will need friends.

Nichomachean Ethics, 1169b4–21[1]

What the erotic lover likes most is the sight of his beloved, and this is the sort of perception he chooses over the others, supposing that this above all is what makes him fall in love and remain in love. In the same way, surely, what friends find most choiceworthy is living together. For friendship is community, and we are related to our friend as we are related to ourselves. Hence, since the perception of our own being is choiceworthy, so is the perception of our friend's being. Perception is active when we live with him; hence, not surprisingly, this is what we seek.

Whatever someone [regards as] his being, or the end for which he chooses to be alive, that is the activity he wishes to pursue in his friend's company. Hence some friends drink together, others play dice, while others do gymnastics and go hunting, or do philosophy. They spend their days together on whatever pursuit in life they like most, since they want to live with their friends, they share the actions in which they find their common life.

Hence the friendship of base people turns out to be vicious. For they are unstable, and share base pursuits; and by becoming similar to each other, they grow vicious. But the friendship of decent people is decent, and increases the more often they meet.

Ibid., 1171b29–1172a12[2]

We ought not to follow the proverb writers and 'think human, since you are human', or 'think mortal, since you are mortal'. Rather, as far as we can, we ought to be pro-immortal, and go to all lengths to live a life that expresses our supreme element; for, however much this element may lack in bulk, by much more does it surpass everything in power and value. Moreover, each person seems to be his understanding, if he is his controlling and better element; it would be absurd then, if he were to choose not his own life but someone else's. And what we have said previously will apply now. For what is proper to each thing's nature is supremely best and pleasantest for it; and hence for a human being the life expressing understanding will be supremely best and pleasantest for it, if understanding above all is the human being. This life, then, will also be happiest.

Ibid., 1177b35–1178a8[3]

Surely it is also absurd to make
the blessed person solitary; for no
one would choose to possess all
good things and yet remain alone,
since a human being is a political
creature, tending by nature to live
with others.

That [the science which investigates first principles and causes] is not a productive science is clear from the history of the earliest philosophers. **For it is from wonder that men both now begin and at first began to philosophize.** Originally even the most obvious difficulties perplexed them, but then, by degrees, they advanced to state difficulties about the profoundest matters – about the phenomena of the moon, the sun and the stars and about the genesis of the universe. And the man who is puzzled believes himself ignorant (hence even the lover of myth is in a sense a lover of wisdom, for myth is woven from wonders). Therefore, since they philosophized in order to escape from ignorance, evidently they were pursuing science for the sake of knowledge itself and not for any practical end. And this is confirmed by the facts: for it was when almost all the necessities of life and the things that make for comfort and recreation were present that such knowledge began to be sought. Evidently then we do not seek knowledge for any ulterior advantage. Rather, as the free man is the one who is defined as existing for himself and not for another, so we pursue this knowledge as the only free science, for it alone exists for itself and for no other end.

Metaphysics, 982b11–28[4]

Evidently we have to acquire knowledge of the first causes (for we say we know each thing only when we think we recognize its first cause) and causes are defined in four ways. In one sense we mean the substance, i.e. the essence . . . in a second the matter or substrate of the thing is meant; in the third, the origin of the movement of the thing, and in a fourth we mean something opposed to this, namely the end for the sake of which movement occurs and change is undergone.

Ibid., 983a24–34[5]

The essence of each thing is what it is said to be in virtue of itself.
There is an essence only of those things whose description is a definition.
The form of each thing is its essence and its primary substance.
I call the essence substance without matter.
Matter is unknowable in itself.
What we seek is the cause, i.e. the form, by reason of which the matter is some definite thing and this is the substance of the thing.
There is knowledge of each thing only when we know its essence.

Ibid., 1029b13–14, 1030a6, 1032b1, 1032b15, 1036a8, 1041b8, 1031b6[6]

For it is from wonder that men both now begin and at first began to philosophize.

As Epicurus says, '**The words of that philosopher who offers no therapy for human suffering are empty and vain.**' For just as there is no use in medical expertise if it does not give therapy for bodily diseases, so too there is no use in philosophy if it does not expel the suffering of the soul.

Porphyry, *To Marcella*, 31[1]

He who has learned the limits of life knows that it is easy to provide that which removes the feeling of pain owing to want and make one's whole life perfect. So there is no need for things which involve struggle.

Principal Doctrines, 21[2]

It is impossible to live pleasantly without living prudently, honourably and justly, and impossible to live prudently, honourably and justly without living pleasantly.

Ibid., 5[3]

If you do not, on every occasion, refer each of your actions to the goal of nature, but instead turn prematurely to some other [criterion] in avoiding or pursuing things, your actions will not be consistent with your reasoning.

Ibid., 25[4]

So when we say that pleasure is the goal, we do not mean the pleasures of the dissipated and those that consist in having a good time, as some out of ignorance and disagreement or refusal to understand suppose we do, but freedom from pain in the body and from disturbance in the soul. For what produces the pleasant life is not continuous drinking and parties or pederasty or womanizing or the enjoyment of fish and other dishes of an expensive table, but sober reasoning which tracks down the causes of every choice and avoidance, and which banishes the opinions which beset souls with the greatest confusion. Of all this the beginning and greatest good is prudence.

Letter to Menoeceus, in Diogenes Laertius, *Lives of the Philosophers*, 10.132[5]

[W]e believe that self-sufficiency is a great good, not in order that we might make do with few things under all circumstances, but so that if we do not have a lot we can make do with few, being genuinely convinced that those who least need extravagance enjoy it most, and that everything natural is easy to obtain and whatever is groundless is hard to obtain, and that simple flavours provide a pleasure equal to that of an extravagant lifestyle when all pain from want is removed, and barley cakes and water provide the highest pleasure when someone in want takes them.

Ibid., 10.130–31[6]

Let no one delay the study of philosophy while young nor weary of it when old. For no one is either too young or too old for the health of the soul. He who says either that the time for philosophy has not yet come or that it has passed is like someone who says that the time for happiness has not yet come or that it has passed. Therefore, both young and old must philosophize, the latter so that although old he may stay young in good things owing to gratitude for what has occurred, the former so that although young he too may be like an old man owing to his lack of fear of what is to come.

Ibid., 10.122[7]

The words of that philosopher
who offers no therapy for human
suffering are empty and vain.

Surely it is worth mentioning Zeno's statement that '**Someone could sooner immerse a bladder filled with air than compel a virtuous man to act against his will.**' For the soul which right reason has braced with true doctrines is unyielding and immovable.

Philo of Alexandria, *On Every Virtuous Man's being Free*, 97[1]

34]

The Stoics say that being happy is the goal for the sake of which everything is done but which is not itself done for the sake of anything. That consists in living according to virtue, in living in agreement, or what is the same, in living in accordance with nature [*physis*]. Zeno defined happiness in this way: Happiness is a good flow of life . . . Yet, they say that while happiness is set up as a target, the end is to obtain happiness, which is the same as being happy.

Stobaeus, *Anthology*, 2.77,16–17[2]

Virtue is a consistent character, choiceworthy for its own sake and not from fear or hope or anything external. Happiness consists in virtue, since virtue is a soul which has been fashioned to achieve consistency in the whole of life.

Diogenes Laertius, *Lives of the Philosophers*, 7.89[3]

'Yes,' the Stoics say, 'but just as in the sea the man at arm's length from the surface is drowning no less than the man who has sunk five hundred fathoms, so even those who are getting close to virtue are no less in a state of vice than those who are far from it.'

Plutarch, *On Common Conceptions of the Stoics*, 1063A–B[4]

The story goes that Zeno was flogging a slave for stealing. 'I was fated to steal,' said the slave. 'And to be flogged,' Zeno replied.

Diogenes Laertius, *Lives of the Philosophers*, 7.23[5]

Someone could sooner immerse a
bladder filled with air than
compel a virtuous man to act
against his will.

Chrysippus rightly says: 'So long as I am unsure about the consequences of any action, I always hold myself to those things which are best suited to secure what conforms with nature, for god himself gave me the power to choose such things. If I knew for certain that it was ordained for me to be sick at this moment, I would welcome the sickness. **If my foot had a brain, it would welcome the mud.**'

Epictetus, *Discourses*, 2.6.9[1]

Diogenes of Babylon said that the purpose of life is 'to act in accordance with good reason in the selection of the things that are in accordance with nature'.

Stobeaus, *Anthology*, 2.76.9–10[2]

According to Cleanthes, all men have a natural tendency to be virtuous.

Ibid., 2.65.8[3]

Chrysippus argues that virtue can be lost on account of intoxication or depression, but Cleanthes holds that it is irremovable, since it is founded on the sound rock of reason.

Diogenes Laertius, *Lives of the Philosophers*, 7.127[4]

All these Stoics agree in taking virtue to be a certain character and power of the soul's commanding faculty . . . a character which is consistent, firm and unalterably rational.

Plutarch, *On Moral Virtue*, 440e–441d[5]

The Stoics say that a man will commit a well-reasoned suicide if he does it on behalf of friends or his country or if he falls victim to unduly severe pain or mutilation or incurable illness.

Diogenes Laertius, *Lives of the Philosophers*, 7.130[6]

How, then, does Chrysippus define courage? 'Courage', he says, 'is scientific knowledge of matters requiring persistence.' Or, 'a tenor of the soul fearlessly obedient to the supreme law in enduring and persisting'. However much we may attack this school, as Carneades used to, I'm afraid that they are the only real philosophers. For which of these definitions does not reveal the tangled conception of courage which lies buried in us all?

Cicero, *Discussions at Tusculum*, 4.24.15[7]

If my foot had a brain, it would welcome the mud.

The natural philosopher Heraclitus tells a story about Hermodorus, a leading man of Ephesus. The fellow-citizens of Hermodorus expelled him from the city: and the philosopher declares that the entire Ephesian population ought to have been deprived of their lives, because the occasion prompted them to make the following thoroughly deplorable announcement: 'No single individual among us', they said, 'must ever be allowed to rise above the rest. Anyone who aspires to such a thing must go and live in another place, among other people.' You get that feeling in every community. **People always hate anyone who is a better man than themselves** . . .

What a lot of trouble one avoids if one refuses to have anything to do with the common herd! To have no job, to direct one's time to literature, is the most wonderful thing in the world. And by literature, I mean the works which give us an opportunity to understand the universe and nature in all its infinity, and the world in which we ourselves live, its sky, land and sea.

Discussions at Tusculum, 5.36.104[1]

Everything which happens in accordance with Nature must be counted among the things which are good.

On Old Age, 19.71[2]

For happiness is to be found not in gaiety, pleasure, laughing, nor in levity – the comrade of jesting: those men are happy, often in sadness, who are constant and steadfast.

On Ends, 2.20.65–6[3]

Whoever disagrees over the sovereign good disagrees over philosophy as a whole.

Ibid., 5.5.14[4]

Remember that the greatest sufferings are cut off by death, that the lesser ones offer us periods of rest; and that we are masters of the moderate ones, so that if they are bearable we shall be able to bear them and if they are not, when life can no longer please us, then we may take our leave of it as from the theatre.

Ibid., 1.15.49[5]

Supposing it were granted to a sage to live in every abundance, his time entirely free to study and reflect upon everything worth knowing; yet if his solitude were such that he could never meet another man he would quit this life.

On Duties, 1.43.153[6]

The fruits of intellect and virtue and of all abundant talents are best employed when shared with one's neighbour.

On Friendship, 19.70[7]

Folly never thinks it has enough, even when it obtains what it desires, but wisdom is happy with what is to hand and is never vexed with itself.

Discussions at Tusculum, 5.18.54[8]

People always hate anyone who is a better man than themselves.

But in this life one finds fear of
    punishment
for evil deeds, fear no less awful
than the deeds themselves, and also
    crimes' expiation:
prison, the dread plummet from the
    high rock,
stripes, torturers, dungeons, red-hot
    tongs,
firebrands, and even if all these are
    spared
the guilty conscience crazed with
    foreboding
applies the scourge and lashes itself,
unable to see any exit from its torment
or release from misery, wild in the terror
that after death there is worse in store.
**In short, fools make their lives a
hell on earth.**
On the Nature of Things, 3.1013–23[1]

By protracting our life we cannot reduce
        one jot
the time we shall spend in death; we've
    not the power
to remit ourselves from death's full
    stretch.
    Ibid., 3.1087–92[2]

Already now, tired and bloated with life,
        nobody bothers
to gaze up at the shining temples of the
    heavens.
    Ibid., 2.1037–8[3]

Don't you know that when you're dead
        there won't be a second you,
standing at your corpse's head, to grieve
    over your demise?
    Ibid., 3.885–6[4]

The funeral dirge is mingled with the
    wail
of the newborn infant hailing the shores
    of light.

No night followed a day and no day a
    night
without someone hearing an infant's
    sickly mewling
mixed with cries of mourners, decked
    out in black.
    Ibid., 2.575–80[5]

Time does not exist in itself, but is
    experienced
only from events which are over and
    done,
or are unfolding now or will follow in
    the future.
No one would have had any notion of
    time apart
from things in flux and stilled things
    around.
    Ibid., 1.459–64[6]

Men work in vain and waste their time
    in empty cares.
And why? Because they fail to see that
    there are
bounds to accumulation and that
    pleasure
can increase only up to a certain point.
Bit by bit their malign dissatisfaction has
    swept
life out to sea and from the depths
has churned up the tides of war.
    Ibid., 5.1430–37[7]

ll2

In short, fools make their lives a
hell on earth.

God is continuously ordering matter through his thought. His thinking was not anterior to his creating and there never was a time when he did not create, the Forms themselves having been with him from the beginning . . . Thus ever thinking he creates and furnishes to sensible things the principle of their existence, so that both should coexist: the ever-creating Divine Mind and the sense-perceptible things to which beginning of being is given.

De Providentia, 1.7[1]

From pre-elemental matter God creates all things, without laying hold of it himself, since it is not lawful for the happy and blessed One to touch limitless chaotic matter. Instead he employs his incorporeal powers, truly designated Forms, so that each genus assumes its fitting shape.

De Specialibus Legibus, 1.328[2]

God, being God, judged in advance that a beautiful copy would never be produced except from a beautiful pattern and that no object of sense would be irreproachable that was not modelled after an archetypal and intelligible idea . . . When a city is being founded to satisfy the vast ambition of some king . . . there comes forward now and then some trained architect who, after studying the climate and the site, first maps out in his mind virtually all the parts of the city that is to be built: temples, gymnasia, market-places, town halls, harbours, houses . . . Accordingly, having received in his soul, as in wax, the impression of each of these objects, he carries in his mind the image of the intelligible city. Then, after awakening these imprints through the innate power of memory, and imprinting their stamp

even deeper, he begins to build the city of stones and timber. Like a good craftsman with his eye trained on the model, he translates each of the incorporeal ideas into physical objects.

Similarly must we think of God. When he was minded to found the Great City, he first conceived the Forms of its parts, out of which he constructed the intelligible world and, using that as his model, he also brought into being the sensible world.

De Opificis Mundi, 16–20[3]

It is fitting for those who have entered into comradeship with knowledge to long to see the truly existing One, but if they are unable to see him, then to see at least his image, the holy *Logos*, and after the *Logos*, its most perfect work in the realm of the sensible, this world. For philosophy was never anything but the earnest desire to see things precisely as they are.

De Confusione Linguarum, 97[4]

God is continuously ordering
matter through his thought.

On many an occasion I felt an urge to cut my life short there and then, and was only held back by the thought of my father, who had been the kindest of fathers to me and was then in his old age. Having in mind how bravely I was capable of dying but how far from bravely he was capable of bearing the loss, I commanded myself to live. **There are times when even to live is an act of bravery.**

Moral Letters to Lucilius, 78[1]

No one dies before their time. The time you leave behind you is no more yours than the time which passed before you were born.

Ibid., 69[2]

As it is with a play, so it is with life – what matters is not how long the acting lasts, but how good it is. It is not important at which point you stop. Stop wherever you will – only make sure that you round it off with a good ending.

Ibid., 77[3]

In the ashes all men are levelled. We're born unequal, we die equal.

Ibid., 91[4]

My own advice to you – not only in the present illness but in your whole life as well – is this: refuse to let the thought of death bother you: nothing is grim when we have escaped that fear.

Ibid., 77[5]

No one has power over us when death is within our own power.

Ibid., 91[6]

Everyone faces up more bravely to a thing for which he has long prepared himself, sufferings, even, being withstood if they have been trained for in advance. Those who are unprepared, on the other hand, are panic-stricken by the most insignificant happenings. We must see to it that nothing takes us by surprise.

Ibid., 107[7]

Philosophy is not an occupation of a popular nature, nor is it pursued for the sake of self-advertisement. Its concern is not with words, but with facts. It is not carried on with the object of passing the day in an entertaining sort of way and taking the boredom out of leisure. It moulds and builds the personality, orders one's life, regulates one's conduct, shows one what one should do and what one should leave undone, sits at the helm and keeps one on the correct course as one is tossed about in perilous seas. Without it no one can lead a life free of fear or worry.

Ibid., 16[8]

There are times when even to live
is an act of bravery.

For we indeed do not all essentially partake of being; but every mortal nature, existing in between generation and corruption, presents only an appearance and an obscure and weak representation of itself . . . so when reason seeks a really clear perception of anything subject to change and decay it is led astray, partly towards generation and partly towards corruption, since it is unable to grasp anything truly enduring or subsisting in it. For we cannot, as Heraclitus says, step into the same river twice, or twice find any perishable substance in the same state . . .
Therefore, whatever is generated does not reach the perfection of being, because genesis never ceases. Always in flux, the seed makes an embryo, then an infant, next comes a child, then a stripling, a youth, a full-grown man, an elderly man and lastly a decrepit old man . . . **We ridiculously fear one death, having died many times already and ceaselessly continuing to die.** For not only, as Heraclitus said, is the death of fire the generation of air, and the death of air the generation of water, but the lesson of change can be learned from men themselves, for when the full-grown man perishes, the old man is born . . . the child dies in the youth, the infant in the child. So yesterday dies in today and today dies in tomorrow.

Of Ei at Apollo's Temple at Delphi[1]

What then is it that really has being?
That which is eternal, ungenerated, incorruptible and unchanging.

Ibid.[2]

We ridiculously fear one death,
having died many times already
and ceaselessly continuing to die.

It is not the things themselves that disturb people but the judgements they make about these things. Death, for instance, is nothing terrible, or else it would have appeared so to Socrates too. But the terror lies in our own judgement about death that death is terrible. So, whenever we are frustrated, or disturbed, or upset, let us never blame others, but only ourselves, that is, our own judgement. It is the action of an uneducated person to lay the blame for his own bad condition upon others; of one who has made a start on his education to lay the blame on himself; and of the one who is fully educated, to blame neither others nor himself.

The Handbook, 5[1]

Do not ask things to happen as you wish, but wish them to happen as they do happen, and your life will run smoothly.

Ibid., 6[2]

Exercise yourself, then, in what is within your power . . . Whoever, then, wants to be free, let him neither want anything, nor avoid anything, which depends on others.

Ibid., 14[3]

If you take on a role that is beyond your powers, you will not only disgrace yourself in that role, but you will neglect the role that you were capable of fulfilling.

Ibid., 37[4]

The condition and character of the layman is that he never expects either benefit or harm from himself, but solely from externals. The condition and character of a philosopher is that he expects all harm and benefit from himself. He has rid himself of all desire; he has transferred his aversion to those things only which are up to us but are contrary to nature. He is moderate in his impulses to all things. If he appears foolish or ignorant, he does not care and, in a word, he keeps guard against himself as his own enemy.

Ibid., 48[5]

When you see someone weeping in sorrow at the departure of his child or the loss of his property, take care not to be carried away by the impression that he is involved in externals that are bad, but at once be ready to say: 'It is not what has happened that afflicts his person . . . but his judgement concerning it.' As far as words go, however, do not shrink from sympathizing with him, and even, if the opportunity arises, from grieving with him; but beware groaning inwardly too.

Ibid., 16[6]

It is not the things themselves that disturb people but the judgements they make about these things.

In relation to each segment of the earth different peoples live in different countries, but if we look at the entire compass of this world there is only one country for all, the whole earth, and one home, the world. Now I am not rushing you into accepting without thought and consideration that what is said is true – I have made no dogmatic statements – but look at everything from all angles and consider it in company with me. One thing only I ask . . . that you do not look at what is written after the fashion of passers-by, or in a spirit of carelessness and boredom, paying but fickle attention to one section after another and then passing on.

The Epicurean Fragment, 25.2.3–11[1]

Indeed the greatly admired 'Republic' of Zeno, who founded the Stoic school, has this one thing as its aim, in short, that we should not live in cities or villages, each group distinguished with its own private justice, but should consider all people our fellow-villagers and fellow-citizens and there should be a single way of life and order as of a herd pastured together and nourished by a common law. Well, Zeno wrote this, having fashioned a dream or image of a philosopher's republic well-ordered by law, but Alexander turned word into deed.

Plutarch, *On the Fortune of Alexander*, 329a–b[2]

We were once distressed by armies, now we are oppressed by laws.

Tacitus, *Annals of Imperial Rome*, 3.25[3]

In relation to each segment of the earth different peoples live in different countries, but if we look at the entire compass of this world there is only one country for all, the whole earth, and one home, the world.

Sceptics are philanthropic and wish to cure by argument, as far as they are able, the conceit and rashness of the Dogmatists. Just as doctors have remedies for bodily afflictions which differ in strength, applying severe remedies to patients who are severely afflicted and milder remedies to those mildly afflicted, so Sceptics propound arguments which differ in strength: they employ weighty arguments, capable of vigorously rebutting the dogmatic affliction of conceit, against those who are distressed by a dangerous rashness, and they use milder arguments against those who are afflicted by a conceit which is superficial and easily cured.

Outlines of Pyrrhonism, 3.32[1]

If, therefore, neither the appearances nor the non-evident things alone are true, nor some appearances true and some non-evident things, nothing is true. If nothing is true, and the criterion seems to need that which is true for judgement, the criterion is useless and empty, even if we should grant as a concession that it has some existence. And indeed if we ought to suspend judgement regarding whether there is something true, it follows that those who say that dialectic is the knowledge of the true and the false and the neutral are being rash.

Ibid., 1.9[2]

So far we have said that the aim of the Sceptic is tranquillity in matters of opinion and moderation of feeling in matters forced upon us. For Sceptics began to do philosophy in order to decide among appearances and to discover which are true and which are false, so as to become tranquil, but they came up against logical impasses in their arguments and, being unable to resolve these, they chose to suspend judgement. And, when they suspended judgement, tranquillity in matters of opinion followed as a fortuitous bonus.

Ibid., 1.12[3]

A story told about the painter Apelles applies to the Sceptics. It is said that he was painting a horse and wanted to depict the froth around the horse's mouth; but he was so unsuccessful that he gave up and taking the sponge on which he had been wiping the colours off his brush he flung it at the painting. And striking the canvas, it produced the living likeness of the horse's froth. Now, the Sceptics were hoping to acquire tranquillity by resolving the anomalies between what appears and what is conceived and, being unable to do this, they suspended judgement and fortuitously found tranquillity in the process.

Ibid., 1.12[4]

Sceptics are philanthropic and
wish to cure by argument, as far
as they are able, the conceit and
rashness of the Dogmatists.

For, I say, God is not external to any one, but is present in all things, though they are oblivious of His presence. For they fly from Him, or rather from themselves. They are unable therefore to apprehend that from which they fly.

'On the Good and the One'[1]

Life in the present severed from God is a vestige of life and a mere imitation of the true life. In contrast, the life in the intelligible world consists in the energy of intellect . . . which generates beauty, justice and virtue. For the soul being filled with God brings forth these, and this is both the beginning and end of the soul. It is her beginning because she originates from there; it is her end because the good is there and when the soul is present in the intelligible realm she becomes what she was before birth.

Ibid.[2]

In the intelligible world . . . the true object of love is to be found, an object pure and fleshless with which we may be united, which we may join with and truly make our own. He, however, who knows this will know what I say and will be convinced that the soul then has another life [beyond the mortal body].

Ibid.[3]

The principle of all things . . . not being differentiated, is ever present; but we are present with it when we too are undifferentiated . . . We perpetually revolve around the principle, although we do not always see it . . . but when we do behold it we obtain the goal of our desires and are stilled. Then we are no longer discordant, but join in a divine dance around the centre of all things.

Ibid.[4]

This, therefore, is the life of the gods and of the divine and happy men: they are liberated from all earthly concerns and live a life unburdened with human pleasures. Their solitary souls fly ceaselessly to the Holy One.

Ibid.[5]

For, I say, God is not external to
any one, but is present in all
things, though they are oblivious
of His presence.

I confess to you, Lord, that I still do not know what time is. Yet I confess too that I do know that I am saying this in time, that I have been talking about time for a long time, and that this long time would not be a long time if it were not for the fact that time has been passing all the while. How can I know this, when I do not know what time is? Is it that I do know what time is, but do not know how to put it into words? **I am in a sorry state, for I do not even know what I do not know!**

Confessions, 11.25[1]

It is in my own mind, then, that I measure time. I must not allow my mind to insist that time is something objective . . . I say that I measure time in my mind. For everything which happens leaves an impression on it, and this impression remains after the thing has ceased to be. It is the impression that I measure, since it is still present, not the thing itself, which makes the impression as it passes and then moves into the past. When I measure time it is the impression that I measure.

Ibid.[2]

Again, no one would deny that the present has no duration, since it exists only for the instant of its passage. Yet the mind's attention persists, and through it that which is to be passes towards the state in which it is to be no more. So it is not future time that is long, but a long future is a long expectation of the future; and past time is not long, because it does not exist, but a long past is a long remembrance of the past.

Ibid.[3]

You, my Father, are eternal. But I am divided between time gone by and time to come, and its course is a mystery to me. My thoughts, the intimate life of my soul, are torn this way and that in the havoc of change. And so it will be until I am purified and melted by the fire of your love and fused into one with you.

Ibid.[4]

Now God is the great artificer in the great things; but that does not mean that he is an inferior artist in the small. For those small things are not to be measured by their size, which is next to nothing, but by the wisdom of their artificer. Take the case of a man's visible appearance. An eyebrow is virtually nothing compared with the whole body; but shave it off and what an immense loss to his beauty! For beauty does not depend on mere size, but on the symmetry and proportion of the component parts.

The City of God, 11.22, 'The Apparent Evil in the Universe'[5]

I am in a sorry state, for I do not
even know what I do not know!

But to return to the pursuits of men. **Despite a clouded memory, the mind seeks its own good, though like a drunkard it cannot find the path home.** No one could say that people who strive to have all they want are wrong. In fact there is no other thing which could so successfully create happiness as a condition provided with all that is good, a condition of self-sufficiency and with no wants . . . It is irrelevant to say that happiness is a condition free from anxiety, sickness and the tyranny of grief and suffering, when even in small matters, what men seek is some thing which gives delight by its possession and enjoyment.

The Consolation of Philosophy[1]

It is clear, therefore, that happiness is a condition made perfect by the presence of everything that is good, a condition which . . . all mortal men are striving to reach by different paths. For desire for true good is implanted by nature in the minds of men, only error leads them astray towards false goals.

Ibid.[2]

Reason shows that God is so good that we are convinced that His goodness is perfect. Otherwise He could not be the author of creation. There would have to be something else possessing perfect goodness over and above God, which would need to be superior to Him and of greater age. For all perfect things are obviously superior to those that are imperfect. Therefore, to avoid an infinite regress, it must be admitted that the supreme God is to the highest degree filled with supreme and perfect goodness. But we have agreed that perfect good is true happiness; so that it follows that true happiness is to be found in the supreme God.

Ibid.[3]

Despite a clouded memory, the mind seeks its own good, though like a drunkard it cannot find the path home.

Something-than-which-a-greater-cannot-be-thought exists so truly, then, that it cannot even be thought not to exist.

And You, Lord our God, are this being. **You exist so truly, Lord my God, that You cannot even be thought not to exist.** And this is as it should be, for if some intelligence could think of something better than You, the creature would be above its creator and would judge its creator – and that is completely absurd. (In fact, everything else there is, except You alone, can be conceived of as not existing.)

Proslogion, 3[1]

No one, indeed, understanding what God is can think that God does not exist, even though he may say these words in his heart either without any meaning or with some peculiar meaning. For God is that-than-which-nothing-greater-than-can-be-thought.

Ibid., 4[2]

Have you found, O my soul, what you were seeking? You were seeking God and you find Him to be something which is the highest of all, something than which a better cannot be thought, and to be life itself, light, wisdom, goodness, eternal blessedness and blessed eternity, and to exist everywhere and always.

Ibid., 14[3]

Truly, Lord, this is the inaccessible light in which You dwell . . . Truly I do not see this light since it is too much for me; and yet whatever I see, I see through it, just as an eye that is weak sees what it sees by the light of the sun which it cannot look at directly . . . You are entirely present everywhere and I do not see You. In You I move and in You I have my being and I cannot come near to You. You are within me and around me and I do not experience You.

Ibid., 16[4]

Therefore, Lord, not only are You that-than-which-a-greater-cannot-be-thought, but You are also something greater than can be thought.

Ibid., 15[5]

You exist so truly, Lord my God, that You cannot even be thought not to exist.

1. God is a monad which gives birth to a monad and reflects its ardour within itself.

2. **God is a sphere whose centre is everywhere, whose circumference is nowhere.**

3. God is wholly complete in every part of himself.

Liber XXIV Philosophorum[1]

If you say that eternity means an existence without end, it must be replied that that does not express the sense of the word eternity since the latter not only means interminability but also simultaneity. You can think of the element of interminability as being like the circumference of a circle which neither begins nor ends, while the element of simultaneity might be compared to the simple and indivisible point which lies at the centre. These two elements are correctly predicated of the Divine Being because He is at once both simple and infinite and also because eternity must be thought of as circular.

Bonaventura, *Quaestiones Disputatae, De Mysterio Trinitatis*, 1.7–8, qu. 5[2]

The divine centre is everywhere since God's virtue has permeated the entirety of nature and exists in every particle of the universe.

Marsilius Ficino, *Tractatus de Deo et Animi Vulgus* (1457)[3]

The entire universe surrounds man as a circle encompasses the point.

Paracelsus, *Explicatio Totius Astronomiae* (1658)[4]

God is a sphere whose centre is everywhere, whose circumference is nowhere.

The sick stand in greater need of assistance and compassion than the fit and strong for three reasons. Firstly, on account of the necessity of sustaining life, which they cannot do for themselves. If the necessities of life are not procured for them by others, they become enfeebled and cannot survive ... Secondly on account of the necessity of restoring health and strength which they have lost by sickness. If even a strong and healthy person needs help to sustain their health, the ailing person needs a two-fold help to restore his strength ... Thirdly on account of the relief that consolation brings ... However, someone says, those for whom there is some hope of recovery are indeed worthy of help, but it is a useless waste to assist those who are hopelessly ill. This would be correct if consideration were shown to the sick for reasons of utility and not charity. But he who comes to the relief of the sick in the hope of receiving a return deprives himself of the satisfaction of charity. **The more hopeless the disease, the more splendid is the devotion and unselfish the charity of those who strive to alleviate it.** It is, therefore, a good thing for a superior occasionally to suffer himself, so he will learn to have compassion for his monks.

Six Wings of the Seraphim[1]

From that time on, Saint Francis clothed himself with a spirit of poverty, a sense of humility and a feeling of intimate devotion. Formerly he used to be horrified not only by close dealings with lepers, but by their very sight, even from a distance; but now he rendered humble service to the lepers with humane concern and devoted kindness in order that he might completely despise himself, because of Christ crucified, who according to the prophet Isaiah was despised as a leper. He visited their houses frequently, generously distributed alms to them and with great compassion kissed their hands and their mouths.

The Life of Saint Francis of Assisi, 1.5–6[2]

True love of God not only seeks to enjoy His sweetness in the closest of unions with Him but also longs to see His will accomplished and due service paid Him and His honour raised on high: it wishes Him to be acknowledged by all and loved and served by all, and honoured above all things.

Six Wings of the Seraphim[3]

The more hopeless the disease,
the more splendid is the devotion
and unselfish the charity of those
who strive to alleviate it.

From the fact that the mind conceives what is meant by the name God, it follows only that God is in the intellect. It is not necessary that that-than-which-nothing-greater-can-be-thought exist anywhere but in the intellect; it does not follow that in reality there exists that-than-which-nothing-greater-can-be-

thought. **There is nothing absurd in denying that God exists.** Nor is it absurd to hold that there can be something greater than whatever be given, in thought or reality, unless one already concedes that-than-which-nothing-greater-can-be-thought exists in reality.

Summa Contra Gentiles, 1.11[1]

The human mind approaches knowledge of God in three ways, though it never attains to knowledge of what he is, but only that he is. First, insofar as his effectiveness in producing things is more perfectly known. Second, insofar as he is known as cause of more noble effects, which since they bear some likeness to him better display his eminence. Third, in this that he is known to be more and more distant from all those things which appear in his effects. Hence Dionysius says in *On the Divine Names* 7 that he is known as the cause, the excess and negation of all things.

The Exposition of Boethius's On the Trinity, 2[2]

Should there be only one doctrine beyond the natural sciences? . . . I reply that on this question it should be noted that knowledge is higher to the degree that it is more unified and extends to more things. Hence, God's intellect, which is highest, has distinct knowledge of all things through something one, which is God himself. So too, divine science is highest and derives its efficacy from the light of divine inspiration itself and, while remaining one and undivided, considers diverse things, and not just universally, like metaphysics, which considers all things insofar as they are beings, without descending to proper knowledge of moral matters or of natural things. Since the notion of being is diversified in diverse things metaphysics is insufficient for specific knowledge of them. But the divine light, remaining one in itself, is efficacious to make them manifest, as Dionysius says at the beginning of the *Celestial Hierarchy*.

Commentary on the Sentences, 1.2[3]

It should be said that man's will is discordant with the will of God insofar as it wills something God does not want it to will, as when it wills to sin; though God does not want the will to will this, if it so wills God brings it about, for whatever it wills the Lord does. And though in this way man's will is discordant with the will of God with respect to the movement of will, it can never be discordant with respect to result or event, for a man's will always chooses that event because God always fulfils his will concerning man. But with respect to the manner of willing it is not necessary that man's will be conformed to God's, because God wills whatever he wills eternally and infinitely, but man does not.

Disputed Question of Evil, 6[4]

There is nothing absurd in
denying that God exists.

It is written: 'They have become rich in all virtues' (1 Corinthians 1:5). Truly, this cannot happen unless they first become poor in all things. **Whoever desires to be given everything must first give everything away.** This is a fair trade and an equal exchange . . . God wishes to give us himself and all things for our own free possession, and therefore he wishes to strip us completely of all that is ours.

Latin Sermons, 23[1]

The freer the mind is, the more powerful and worthy, the more useful, praiseworthy and perfect the prayer and the work become. A free mind can achieve all things. But what is a free mind?

A free mind is one which is untroubled and unfettered by anything, which has not bound its best part to any particular manner of being or worship and which does not seek its own interest in anything but is always immersed in God's most precious will, having gone out of what is its own. There is no work which men and women can perform, however small, which does not draw from this its power and strength.

Ibid., 2[2]

We must learn to free ourselves of ourselves in all our gifts, not holding on to what is our own or seeking anything, either profit, pleasure, inwardness, sweetness, reward, heaven or your own will. God never gives himself, or ever has given himself, to a will that is alien to himself, but only to his own will. Where he finds his own will, he gives himself and enters in with all that he is. And the more we cease to be in our own will, the more truly we begin to be in God's will. Thus it is not enough for us

to give ourselves up just once, together with all we have and are capable of, but we must renew ourselves constantly, thus preserving our freedom and simplicity in all things.

Ibid., 21[3]

The more perfect and pure the powers of the soul are, the more perfectly and comprehensively they can receive the object of their perception, embracing and experiencing a greater bliss, and the more they become one with that which they perceive, to such a degree indeed that the highest power of the soul, which is free of all things and which has nothing in common with anything else at all, perceives nothing less than God himself in the breadth and fullness of his being.

The Book of Divine Consolation[4]

The just person seeks nothing through their works, for those whose works are aimed at a particular end or who act with a particular Why in view are servants and hirelings. If you wish to be formed and transformed into justice, then, do not intend anything particular by your works and do not embrace any particular Why, neither in time nor in eternity, neither reward nor blessedness, neither this nor that; such works in truth are dead. Indeed, even if you make God your goal, all the works you perform for his sake will be dead, and you will only spoil those works which are genuinely good . . . If your works are to be living works, then God must spur you to action from your innermost part, if they really are to be alive.

German Sermon, 10[5]

Whoever desires to be given
everything must first give
everything away.

The reason why the saints and others say that God is His very existence is this. **God exists in such a manner that He cannot not exist; in fact, He exists necessarily; and He is not from something else.**

Summa Totius Logicae, 3.2.127[1]

Nothing must be affirmed without a reason being assigned for it, except it be something known by itself, known by experience, or if it be something proved by the authority of holy scripture.

Ordinatio, d. 30, qu. 1.E[2]

We must not affirm that something is necessarily required for the explanation of an effect, if we are not led to this by a reason proceeding either from a truth known by itself or from an experience that is certain.

Reportatio, 2, qu. 150[3]

What can be explained by the assumption of fewer things is vainly explained by the assumption of more things.

Ibid., qu. 254[4]

If . . . in the proposition 'This is an angel' subject and predicate stand for the same thing the proposition is true. Hence it is not denoted, by this proposition, that this [individual] has 'angelity' or that 'angelity' is in him, or something of that kind, but it is denoted that this [individual] is truly an angel. Not indeed that he is this predicate ['angel'] but that he is that for which the predicate stands. In like manner also, the propositions 'Socrates is a man', 'Socrates is an animal', do not denote that Socrates has humanity or animality, nor that humanity or animality is in Socrates, nor that man or animal belongs to the essence or quiddity of Socrates or to the quidditative concept of Socrates. They rather denote that Socrates is truly a man and that he is truly an animal; not that Socrates is the predicate 'man' or the predicate 'animal', but that he is something that the predicate 'man' and the predicate 'animal' stand for or represent; for each of these predicates stands for Socrates.

Summa Totius Logicae, 2.3.2[5]

A real science is not about things, but about mental contents standing for things, for the terms of scientifically known propositions stand for things. Hence in the following scientifically known proposition, 'All fire is warming', the subject is a mental content common to every fire, and stands for every fire.

Prologue to *Expositio super VIII Libros Physicorum*[6]

It is vain to do by many means what can be done by one.

Odo Rigaldus, *Commentarius super Sententias*, MS Bruges 208, fol. 150a[7]

God exists in such a manner that He cannot not exist; in fact, He exists necessarily; and He is not from something else.

After doctors, next place [among popular folly's favourites] must be given to shyster lawyers – indeed, I'm not sure they shouldn't occupy first position, since, setting my own opinion aside, the philosophers have agreed in overwhelming numbers to ridicule their profession as asinine. Yet, asses though they are, great matters and small alike are settled by the judgements of these men. By their means and for their benefit great fortunes are amassed while the theologian, having struggled through all his volumes of divinity, dines on beans and wages war on bugs and black beetles. **Thus it appears those arts are most blessed which have the closest affinity with stupidity, and those people are happiest who have been able to avoid contact with the arts and sciences altogether, simply following nature, which never fails them except when they try to reach beyond the proper limits of their human nature.** False faces are odious to nature, and a man gets ahead much faster if he does without artifice.

The Praise of Folly[1]

It's utter misery, the philosophers say, to be in the clutches of folly, to be bewildered, to blunder, to never know anything for sure. On the contrary, I say, that's what it is to be a man. I don't see why they should call that condition miserable into which we were born, in which we were bred, in which we have grown up – which is the common fate of every one of us. There's nothing miserable about what conforms with one's basic nature – unless someone wants to argue that man should be considered wretched because he can't fly

with the birds . . . or threaten his foes with horns like the bull.

Ibid.[2]

But a writer of my school cultivates a much happier vein of craziness, since he takes no care of his work, but just pops down whatever pops into his head or slips off his pen, even his dreams. He knows perfectly well the sillier the nonsense the more it will appeal to a mass audience, who are almost all fools and blockheads . . . Smarter yet are those who adopt the writings of others as their own, easily transforming another man's hard work to their own account and cheered with the pleasant thought that, even if they're convicted of plagiarism, they will have been able to coin plenty of money in the meantime.

Ibid.[3]

Lord Almighty, what a theatre this is, what a wild storm of follies!

Ibid.[4]

Thus it appears those arts are most blessed which have the closest affinity with stupidity, and those people are happiest who have been able to avoid contact with the arts and sciences altogether, simply following nature, which never fails them except when they try to reach beyond the proper limits of their human nature.

I conclude, therefore, that as fortune is changeable and men are obstinate in their ways, men prosper so long as fortune and policy are in accord. **I do hold strongly to this: that it is better to be rash rather than timid; for Fortune is a woman and the man who wants to subdue her must beat and bully her.** Experience shows that she is more often won by impetuous men than by men who proceed coldly. And also, like a woman, she favours young men, because they are less timid and more ardent and command her with greater audacity.

The Prince, 25[1]

Nevertheless, because free choice cannot be ruled out, I believe that it is probably true that fortune is arbiter of about half the things we do, leaving the other half to ourselves. I compare fortune to one of those violent rivers which, when they are enraged, flood the plains, tear down trees and buildings, wash soil from one place and deposit it in another. Everyone flees before them, everyone yields to their impetus, there is no possibility of resistance. Yet although such is their nature, it does not follow that, when they are flowing quietly, one cannot take precautions constructing embankments and dykes so that when the river is in flood it runs into a canal or else its impetus is less wild and dangerous. So it is with fortune. She shows her power where there is no force to hold her in check: and her impetus is felt where she knows there are no dykes or embankments built to restrain her.

Ibid.[2]

I have often thought that the reasons why men are sometimes unfortunate, sometimes fortunate, depends upon whether their behaviour is in conformity with the times. For one sees that in what they do some men are impetuous, others look about them and are cautious; and that, since in both cases they go to extremes and are unable to go about things in the right way, in both cases they make mistakes. But he will err least and be the most favoured by fortune who adjusts his conduct to suit the times and acts in accord with the force of nature.

Discourses on Livy, 3.9[3]

A Republic has a fuller life and enjoys good fortune for a longer time than a principality, since it is better able to adapt itself to diverse circumstances owing to the diversity found among its citizens than a prince can do. For a man who is accustomed to act in one particular way, never changes . . . Hence, when times change, and no longer suit his ways, he is inevitably ruined.

Ibid.[4]

I do hold strongly to this: that it is
better to be rash rather than
timid; for Fortune is a woman
and the man who wants to
subdue her must beat and bully
her.

That diversifying of tongues and languages by which God threw confusion over the enterprise of Babel, what else does it signify if not the infinite, endless altercation over discordant opinions and arguments which accompanies the vain structures of human knowledge, enmeshing them in confusion. Usefully enmeshing them! **If we actually possessed one grain of knowledge, there would be no holding us back.**

'An Apology for Raymond Sebond'[1]

Nature, being equal and common to all, cannot fail to be just. But since we have unslaved ourselves from Nature's law and given ourselves over to the vagrant liberty of our mental perceptions, the least we can do is to help ourselves by making them incline in the most agreeable direction.

'The Taste for Good and Evil Things Depends on our Opinion'[2]

Nature clasps all her creatures in a universal embrace; there is not one of them which she has not plainly furnished with all means necessary to the conservation of its being.

'An Apology for Raymond Sebond'[3]

But seriously though, is not Man a wretched creature? Because of his natural attributes he is hardly able to taste one single pleasure pure and entire; yet he has to go and curtail even that by arguments; he is not wretched enough until he has increased his wretchedness by art and assiduity.

'On Moderation'[4]

From similar effects we should conclude that there are similar faculties. Consequently, we should admit that animals employ the same method and the same reasoning as ourselves when we do anything. Why should we think that they have inner natural instincts different from anything we experience in ourselves? Added to which, it is more honourable that we be guided towards regular, obligatory behaviour by the natural and ineluctable properties of our being; that is more God-like than rash and fortuitous freedom; it is safer to leave the driver's reins in Nature's hands not ours.

'An Apology for Raymond Sebond'[5]

I find . . . that there is nothing savage or barbarous about those peoples [cannibals], but that every man calls barbarous anything he is not accustomed to; it is indeed the case that we have no other criterion of truth or right-reason than the example and form of the opinions and customs of our own country.

'On the Cannibals'[6]

Now laws remain respected not because they are just but because they are laws. That is the mystical basis of their authority. They have no other . . . Laws are often made by fools, and even more often by men who fail in equity because they hate equality: but always by men, vain authorities who can resolve nothing.

'On Experience'[7]

Nature brought us free and unbound: we imprison ourselves in particular confines, like those kings of Persia who bind themselves to drink no water but that of the river Choaspes, foolishly renouncing their right to use all other waters, making, so far as they are concerned, all the rest of the world a desert.

'On Vanity'[8]

If we actually possessed one grain
of knowledge, there would be no
holding us back.

As long as a man clings to a place he clings to distinction. Hence I pray to God to set me free for that absolutely purified being which exists above God and above distinction. I was once in that purified being and there I thought and willed myself to be this man I am. Hence, I am the creation of both my eternal and my temporal being. I was born into temporal life, but because of my eternal birth I can never die. Thanks to my eternal birth I have always been, am now and shall always be. My temporal being shall pass away and come to nought, for it is meant to last for only a time. But in my eternal birth all things were brought forth. I was the cause of myself and all things. Indeed, had I so willed, I and all things would not yet be. **Were I not, God would not be.**

Von waarer Armut des Geistes oder gelassener Gelassenheit[1]

All knowledge of divine things comes forth from man himself and not from books.

Der Güldene Griff, Theologia Weigelia (Frankfurt, 1699) A.6.b[2]

The learned with their books, Scripture and scholarship are far from the kingdom of God. They are so crammed with arts and sciences that God cannot find a space the size of a pinhead to work within them.

Ibid., J.2.a[3]

All wisdom and knowledge of truth are pre-existent in man and do not come to him from external objects.

Ibid., D.2.b[4]

Were I not, God would not be.

The gems of philosophy are not less precious because they are not understood. With all our power we must defend them and help them defend themselves and us, liberate them and save them from being trampled under the feet of the hogs . . . '[M]y so beloved mother philosophy' . . . is reduced to such a state that among the common people a philosopher is tantamount to an impostor, an idler, a common pedant, a faker, a charlatan . . . True philosophers, however, even though they have been elevated from humble backgrounds, cannot help but become ennobled and civilized because knowledge is an excellent way to make the human soul heroic.

Concerning the Cause, Principle and One, 1[1]

It is not reasonable to believe that any part of the whole is without a soul-life, sensation and organic structure. From this infinite All, full of beauty and splendour, from the worlds which circle above us, to the sparkling dust of the world beyond, the conclusion is drawn that there are an infinity of creatures; a vast multitude which, each in its own degree, mirrors forth the splendour, wisdom and excellence of the divine beauty.

The Expulsion of the Triumphant Beast[2]

None of our sense perceptions are opposed to the acceptance of infinity, since we cannot deny infinity merely because we do not sensibly perceive it; but since sense itself is included in infinity, and since reason does not confine infinity, therefore infinity must be posited. Moreover, careful consideration reveals that sense does present to us an infinite universe. For we perceive an endless series of objects, each one contained by another, and we never perceive, either through our internal or external sense, an object which is not contained by a different or similar object.

On the Infinite Universe and Worlds[3]

It has not been vainly said that Jove fills all things, inhabits all parts of the universe, is the centre of all that has being – one is all, and all is one. The One, being all things and comprising all being, brings it about that everything exists in everything.

Concerning the Cause, Principle and One, 5[4]

To a body of infinite size neither centre nor boundary can be ascribed . . . Just as we regard ourselves at the centre of that universally equidistant circle which is the great horizon of our encircling, ethereal region, so doubtless the inhabitants of the moon believe themselves to be at the centre of a circle that embraces the earth, the sun and the stars and is the boundary of their own horizon. Thus the earth no more than any other world is at the centre.

On the Infinite Universe and Worlds[5]

80]

The gems of philosophy are not
less precious because they are not
understood.

It is idle to expect any great advance in science from the old superinducing and engrafting of new things upon old. **We must begin again from the very foundations, unless we would revolve for ever in a circle with mean and contemptible progress.**

Novum Organum, 1.31[1]

One method of delivery alone remains to us; which is simply this: we must lead men to the particulars themselves, and to their series and order; while men on their side must force themselves to lay their notions aside for a while and begin to familiarize themselves with facts.

Ibid., 1.36[2]

The human understanding is of its own nature prone to abstractions, and gives a substance and reality to things which are fleeting . . . Matter rather than forms should be the object of our attention, its configurations and changes of configuration, and its simple action, and the laws of action or motion; for forms are figments of the human mind, unless you call those laws of action forms.

Ibid., 1.51[3]

But if a man endeavours to establish and extend the power and dominion of the human race itself over the universe, his ambition . . . is without doubt both a more wholesome thing and a more noble thing than the others. Now the empire of man over things depends wholly on the arts and the sciences. For we cannot command nature except by obeying her.

Ibid., 1.129[4]

I had rather believe all the fables in the Legend, and the Talmud, and the Alcoran, than that this universal frame is without a mind. And therefore God never wrought miracle to convince atheism, because his ordinary works convince it. It is true, that a little philosophy inclineth a man's mind to atheism; but depth in philosophy bringeth men's minds about to religion: for while the mind of man looketh upon second causes scattered, it may sometimes rest in them, and go no further; but when it beholdeth the chain of them confederate and linked together, it must needs fly to Providence and Deity.

'Of Atheism'[5]

Some books are to be tasted, others to be swallowed, and some few to be chewed and digested . . . Some books also may be read by deputy, and extracts made of them by others; but that would be only in the less important arguments, and the meaner sort of books; else distilled books are like common distilled waters, flashy things.

'Of Studies'[6]

We must begin again from the very foundations, unless we would revolve for ever in a circle with mean and contemptible progress.

So that in the right Definition of Names, lies the first use of speech: which is the Acquisition of Science: And in wrong, or no Definitions, lies the first abuse; from which proceed all false and senseless Tenets; which make those men that take their instruction from the authority of books, and not from their own meditation, to be as much below the condition of ignorant men, as men endued with true Science are above it. For between true Science, and erroneous Doctrines, Ignorance is in the middle. Natural sense and imagination are not subject to absurdity. Nature itself cannot err: and as men abound in copiousness of language; so they become more wise, or more mad than ordinary. Nor is it possible without Letters for any man to become either excellently wise, or (unless his memory be hurt by disease, or ill constitution of organs) excellently foolish. **For words are wise men's counters, they do but reckon by them; but they are the money of fools, that value them by the authority of an _Aristotle_, a _Cicero_, or a _Thomas_, or any other Doctor whatsoever, if but a man.**

Leviathan, 1.4, 'Necessity of Definitions'[1]

And when men think themselves wiser than all others, clamour and demand right Reason for judge; yet, seek no more, but that things should be determined, by no other men's reason but their own, it is as intolerable in the society of men, as it is in play after trump is turned, to use for trump on every occasion, that suit whereof they have the most in their hand. For they do nothing else, that will have every of their passions, as it comes to bear sway in them, to be taken for right Reason, and that in their own controversies:

bewraying their want of right Reason, by the claim they lay to it.

Ibid., 1.5, 'Right Reason where'[2]

Whatsoever accidents or qualities our senses make us think there be in the world, they are not there, but are seemings and apparitions only. The things that really are in the world without us, are those motions by which these seemings are caused. And this is the great deception of sense, which also is by sense to be corrected. For as sense telleth me, when I see directly, that the colour seemeth to be in the object; so also sense telleth me, when I see by reflection, that colour is not in the object.

The Elements of Law, 1.2.10[3]

For words are wise men's counters, they do but reckon by them; but they are the money of fools, that value them by the authority of an *Aristotle*, a *Cicero*, or a *Thomas*, or any other Doctor whatsoever, if but a man.

Every man, for his own part, calleth that which pleaseth, and that is delightful to himself, GOOD; and that EVIL which displeaseth him: insomuch that while every man differeth from other in constitution, they differ also from another concerning the common distinction of good and evil. Nor is there any such thing as ἀγαθὸν ἀπλῶς [*agathon haplos*] that is to say, simply good. For even the goodness which we attribute to God Almighty, is his goodness to us. And as we call good and evil the things that please and displease us; so call we goodness and badness, the qualities of powers whereby they do it.

The Elements of Law, 1.7.3[4]

In the state of nature, where every man is his own judge, and differeth from others concerning the names and appellations of things, and from those differences arise quarrels, and breach of peace; it was necessary there should be a common measure of all things that might fall in controversy; as for example: of what is to be called right, what good, what virtue, what much, what little . . . etc. For in these things private judgements may differ and beget controversy. This common measure, some say, is right reason: with whom I should consent if there was any such thing to be found or known *in rerum natura*. But commonly they that call for right reason to decide any controversy do mean their own. But this is certain, seeing right reason is not existent, the reason of some man, or men, must supply the place thereof . . .

Ibid., 2.10.8[5]

Hereby it is manifest, that during the time men live without a common power to keep them all in awe, they are in that condition which is called war; and such a war, as is of every man, against every man.

Leviathan, 1.13, 'Out of civil states there is always *War* of everyone against everyone'[6]

And because the condition of Man . . . is a condition of every one against every one; in which every one is governed by his own Reason; and there is nothing he can make use of, that may not be a help unto him, in preserving his life against his enemies; it followeth, that in such a condition, every man has a right to everything; even to one another's body. And therefore, as long as this natural Right of every man to everything endureth, there can be no security to any man (how strong or wise soever he be) of living out the time, which Nature ordinarily alloweth men to live. And consequently it is a precept, or general rule of Reason, *That every man, ought to endeavour Peace, as far as he has hope of obtaining it; and when he cannot obtain it, that he may seek, and use, all helps, and advantages of war.*

Ibid., 1.14, 'Naturally every man has Right to everything'[7]

Every man, for his own part, calleth that which pleaseth, and that is delightful to himself, GOOD; and that EVIL which displeaseth him: insomuch that while every man differeth from other in constitution, they differ also from another concerning the common distinction of good and evil.

In the matters we propose to investigate, our inquiries should be directed, not to what others have thought, nor to what we ourselves conjecture, but to what we can clearly and distinctly see and with certainty deduce, for knowledge is not won in any other
way.

To study the writings of the ancients is right because it is a great boon for us to be able to make use of the labours of so many men; and we should do so, both in order to discover what they have correctly made out in previous ages, and also that we may inform ourselves as to what in the various sciences is still left for investigation. But yet there is a great danger lest in a too absorbed study of these works we should become infected with their errors, guard against them as we may.

Rules for the Direction of the Mind, 3[1]

Method consists entirely in the order and disposition of the objects towards which our mental vision must be directed if we would find out any truth. We shall comply with it exactly if we reduce involved and obscure propositions step by step to those that are simpler and then, starting with intuitive apprehension of all those that are absolutely simple, attempt to ascend to the knowledge of all others by precisely similar steps.

In this alone lies the sum of all human endeavour, and he who would approach the investigation of truth must hold to this rule as closely as he who enters the labyrinth must follow the thread which guided Theseus.

Ibid., 5[2]

Although my nature is such that, as long as I perceive something very clearly and distinctly, I am unable not to believe that it is true, my nature is also such that I cannot fix my mind's eye always on the same thing in order to perceive it clearly, and the memory of an earlier judgement often returns when I am no longer considering the reasons why I made that judgement. Thus other reasons would occur to me, if I was ignorant of God, which would easily make me change my mind and in that way I would never have true and certain knowledge about anything but merely unstable and changeable opinions . . .

But once I perceived that God exists and have also understood, at the same time, that everything else depends on him and that he is not a deceiver, I concluded that all those things that I clearly and distinctly perceive are necessarily true.

Meditations on First Philosophy, 6[3]

All young people, in fact, seek truth when they first apply themselves to the study of philosophy. All others also, of whatever age, seek it when they meditate alone on the matters of philosophy and examine them for their own use. Even the princes and magistrates and all those who establish academies . . . and furnish great sums for the teaching of philosophy in them are quite unanimous in desiring that as far as possible only true philosophy should be taught. . . . For there never has been a people so savage or barbarous, or one which shrinks so much from the right use of reason which is the province of men alone, as to let opinions contrary to the known truth be taught in its midst.

Letter to Father Dinet[4]

In the matters we propose to
investigate, our inquiries should
be directed, not to what others
have thought, nor to what we
ourselves conjecture, but to what
we can clearly and distinctly see
and with certainty deduce, for
knowledge is not won in any
other way.

Neither the sun nor death can be looked at steadily.
  Maxims, 26[1]

Few men know death. They usually don't undergo it resolutely but stupidly and out of habit; and the majority of men die because men cannot help themselves dying.
  Ibid., 23[2]

We are led to our duty out of our laziness and timidity, but often our virtue gets all the credit.
  Ibid., 169[3]

Nobody deserves to be praised for goodness unless he is strong enough to be bad, for any other goodness is usually merely inertia or lack of will.
  Ibid., 237[4]

Moderation cannot take credit for combating and subjugating ambition, for the two things are never found together. Moderation is languor and idleness of the soul, ambition is its activity and energy.
  Ibid., 293[5]

We are so biased in our own favour that often what we take for virtues are only vices disguised by self-love.
  Ibid., 607[6]

The scorn for riches displayed by the philosophers was a secret desire to recompense their own merit for the injustice of Fortune by scorning those very benefits she had denied them; it was a secret way of making sure they were free from poverty's taint, a devious path towards the respect they could not command by wealth.
  Ibid., 54[7]

Social life would not last long if men were not duped by one another.
  Ibid., 87[8]

Old people are fond of giving good advice; it consoles them for no longer being capable of setting a bad example.
  Ibid., 93[9]

Neither the sun nor death can be looked at steadily.

Man's greatness comes from knowing he is wretched: a tree does not know it is wretched.

Thus it is wretched to know that one is wretched, but there is greatness in knowing one is wretched.

Pensées, 114[1]

All our life passes in this way: we seek rest by struggling against certain obstacles, and once they are overcome, rest proves intolerable because of the boredom it produces. We must get away from it and crave excitement.

We think either of present or of threatened miseries, and even if we felt quite safe on every side, boredom on its own would not fail to emerge from the depths of our hearts, where it is naturally rooted, and poison our whole mind.

Man is so unhappy that he would be bored even if he had no cause for boredom, by the very nature of his temperament, and he is so vain that, though he has a thousand and one basic reasons for being bored, the slightest thing, like pushing a ball with a billiard cue, will be enough to divert him.

Ibid., 136[2]

If our condition were truly happy we should not need to divert ourselves from thinking about it.

Ibid., 70[3]

Anyone who does not see the vanity of the world is very vain himself. So who does not see it, apart from young people whose lives are all noise, diversions, and thoughts for the future?

But take away their diversion and you will see them bored to extinction. Then they feel their nullity without recognizing it, for nothing could be more wretched than to be intolerably depressed as soon as one is reduced to introspection with no means of diversion.

Ibid., 36[4]

Thinking reed. It is not in space that I must seek my human dignity, but in the ordering of my thought. It will do me no good to own land. Through space the universe grasps me and swallows me up like a speck; through thought I grasp it.

Ibid., 113[5]

Diversion. It is easier to bear death when one is not thinking about it than the idea of death when there is no danger.

Ibid., 72[6]

Man's greatness comes from
knowing he is wretched: a tree
does not know it is wretched.

Diversity is Pleasant

**The more we let each voice sing
    out with its own true tone,
the richer will be the diversity of
    the chant in unison.**

The Cherubinic Wanderer, 1.268[1]

A heart which is content in time and
    space
does not know its own vastness.
    Ibid., 3.112[2]

I do not know what I am:
I am not what I know.
    Ibid., 1.5[3]

With God All Things are One
To God the croaking frog chorus sounds
    as fair
as the lark's sweet trill, thrilling in the
    air.
    Ibid., 1.269[4]

God is pure absence, unfixed by time or
    space,
The more you seek Him, the more He
    escapes.
    Ibid., 1.25[5]

A Heart Can Enclose God
The Most High is without measure,
    unspeakably immense,
and yet a human heart can completely
    Him embrace.
    Ibid., 3.135[6]

The more we let each voice sing
   out with its own true tone,
the richer will be the diversity of
   the chant in unison.

PROPOSITION 48. **In the mind there is no absolute, or free, will; but the mind is determined to will this or that by a cause which is likewise determined by another, and this again by another, and so on to infinity.**

Proof. The mind is a certain and determinate mode of thinking (by Proposition 11, Part 2), and so (by Corollary 2, Proposition 17, Part 1) cannot be the free cause of its own actions, *or*, cannot have an absolute faculty of willing and not willing. Rather, it must be determined to will this or that (Proposition 28, Part 1) by a cause which is determined by another, and this again by another, and so on. *Q.e.d.*

Ethics, Part 2[1]

Nothing happens in Nature which can be attributed to any defect in it, for Nature is always the same, and its virtue and power of acting are everywhere one and the same; that is, the laws and rules of Nature, according to which all things happen, and change from one form to another, are everywhere and always the same. So the way of understanding the nature of anything must also be the same; namely, through the universal laws and rules of Nature. Therefore the emotions of hatred, anger, envy, etc., considered in themselves, follow from the same necessity and force of Nature as all other particular things. So these emotions are assignable to definite causes through which they can be understood, and have definite properties, equally deserving of our investigation as the properties of any other thing, whose mere contemplation affords us pleasure.

Ibid., Part 3, Preface[2]

No one as yet has determined what the body can do, that is, experience has not yet taught anyone what the body can do by the laws of Nature alone, insofar as Nature is only considered to be corporeal, and what the body can do only if it is determined by the mind. For no one yet has come to know the structure of the body so accurately as to explain all its functions – not to mention that many things are observed among the lower animals which far surpass human ingenuity, and that sleepwalkers do many things in their sleep which they would not dare when awake. This shows well enough that the body, solely from the laws of its own nature, can do many things which its mind wonders at.

Ibid., Part 3, prop. 2, scholium[3]

A baby thinks that it freely seeks milk, an angry child that it freely seeks revenge, and a timid man that he freely seeks flight . . . So experience itself, no less clearly than reason, teaches that men believe themselves to be free because they are conscious of their own actions and ignorant of the causes by which they are determined; and it teaches us too that the decisions of the mind are nothing but the appetites themselves, which therefore vary as the disposition of the body varies. For each man's actions are shaped by his emotion; and those who furthermore are a prey to conflicting emotions know not what they want, while those who are free from emotion are driven on to this or that course by the slightest impulses.

Ibid.[4]

In the mind there is no absolute, or free, will; but the mind is determined to will this or that by a cause which is likewise determined by another, and this again by another, and so on to infinity.

[T]hey make the soul and the man two persons, who make the soul think apart from what the man is conscious of. For, I suppose, nobody will make identity of persons to consist in the soul's being united to the very same numerical particles of matter. For if that be necessary to identity, it will be impossible, in that constant flux of particles of our bodies, that any man should be the same person two days, or two moments together.

13. Thus, methinks, every drowsy nod shakes their doctrine who teach that the soul is always thinking. Those, at least, who do at any time sleep without dreaming can never be convinced that their thoughts are sometimes for four hours busy without their knowing of it . . .

15. **To think often and never to retain it so much as one moment is a very useless sort of thinking; and the soul in such a state of thinking does very little if at all excel that of a looking-glass, which constantly receives variety of images or *ideas* but retains none: they disappear and vanish and there remain no footsteps of them; the looking-glass is never the better for such *ideas*, nor the soul for such thoughts** . . . Nature never makes excellent things for mean or no uses; and it is hardly to be conceived that our infinitely wise Creator should make so admirable a faculty as the power of thinking, that faculty which comes nearest the excellency of his own incomprehensible being, to be so idly and uselessly employed, at least one-fourth part of its time here, as to think constantly without remembering any of those thoughts, without doing any good to itself or others or being in any way useful to any other part of creation.

An Essay Concerning Human Understanding, 2.1, 'Of Ideas in General and their Original'[1]

17. I pretend not to teach but to inquire; and therefore cannot but confess here again that external and internal sensation are the only passages that I can find of knowledge to the understanding. These alone, as far as I can discover, are the windows by which light is let into this *dark room*.

Ibid., 2.11, 'Of Discerning, and Other Operations of the Mind'[2]

17. The chief end of language in communication being to be understood, words serve not well for that end, neither in civil nor philosophical discourse, when any word does not excite in the hearer the same *idea* which it stands for in the mind of the speaker. Now, since sounds have no natural connexion with our *ideas*, but have all their signification from the arbitrary imposition of men, the *doubtfulness* and uncertainty of *their signification* . . . has its cause more in the *ideas* they stand for than in any incapacity there is in one sound more than in another to signify any *idea*, for in that regard they are all equally perfect.

Ibid., 3.9, 'Of the Imperfection of Words'[3]

To think often and never to retain it so much as one moment is a very useless sort of thinking; and the soul in such a state of thinking does very little if at all excel that of a looking-glass, which constantly receives variety of images or *ideas* but retains none: they disappear and vanish and there remain no footsteps of them; the looking-glass is never the better for such *ideas*, nor the soul for such thoughts.

10. It follows from the supreme perfection of God that he chose the best possible plan in producing the universe, a plan in which there is the greatest variety together with the greatest order. The most carefully used plot of ground, place and time; the greatest effect produced by the simplest means; the most power, knowledge, happiness, and goodness in created things that the universe could allow. For, since all the possibles have a claim to existence in God's understanding in proportion to their perfections, the result of all these claims must be the most perfect actual world possible. And without this, it would not be possible to give a reason for why things have turned out in this way rather than otherwise.

Principles of Nature and Grace, Based on Reason[1]

13. For everything is ordered in things once and for all, with as much order and agreement as possible, since supreme wisdom and goodness can only act with perfect harmony: the present is pregnant with the future; the future can be read in the past; the distant is expressed in the proximate. One could know the beauty of the universe in each soul, if one could unfold all its folds, which only open perceptibly with time. But since each distinct perception of the soul includes an infinity of confused perceptions which embrace the whole universe, the soul itself knows the things it perceives only in so far as it has distinct and heightened [*révélées*] perceptions; and it has perfection to the extent that it has distinct perceptions. Each soul knows the infinite – knows all – but confusedly. It is like walking on the seashore and hearing the great noise of the sea: I hear the particular noises of

each wave, of which the whole noise is composed, but without distinguishing them.

Ibid.[2]

63. The body belonging to a monad (which is the entelechy or soul of that body) together with an entelechy constitutes what may be called a *living being*, and together with a soul constitutes what is called an *animal*. Now, the body of a living being or an animal is always organized; for, since every monad is a mirror of the universe in its way, and since the universe is regulated in a perfect order, there must also be an order in the representing being, that is, in the perceptions of the soul, and consequently, in the body in accordance with which the universe is represented therein.

64. Thus each organized body of a living being is a kind of divine machine or natural automaton, which infinitely surpasses all artificial automata. For a machine constructed by man's art is not a machine in each of its parts. For example, the tooth of a brass wheel has parts or fragments which, for us, are no longer artificial things, and no longer have any marks to indicate the machine for whose use the wheel was intended. But natural machines, that is, living bodies, are still machines in their least parts, to infinity. This is the difference between nature and art, that is, between divine art and our art.

The Monadology[3]

It follows from the supreme perfection of God that he chose the best possible plan in producing the universe, a plan in which there is the greatest variety together with the greatest order.

703. Now, since the minds of the first men of the gentile world took things one at a time, being in this respect little better than the minds of beasts, for which each new sensation cancels the last one (which is the cause of their being unable to compare and reason discursively) therefore their sentences must all have been formed in the singular by those who felt them . . .

704. **Abstract sentences are the work of philosophers, because they contain universals, but reflections on the passions are the work of false and frigid poets.**

The New Science (1744 edition), 2.7.3[1]

161. There must in the nature of human institutions be a mental language common to all nations, which uniformly grasps the substance of things feasible in human social life and expresses it with as many diverse modifications as these same things may have diverse aspects. A proof of this is afforded by proverbs or maxims of vulgar wisdom, in which substantially the same meanings find as many diverse expressions as there are nations ancient and modern.

Ibid., 1.12.22[2]

144. Uniform ideas originating among entire peoples unknown to each other must have a common ground of truth.

145. This axiom is a great principle which establishes the common sense of the human race as the criterion taught to the nations by divine providence to define what is certain in the natural law of the nations. And the nations reach this certainty by recognizing the underlying agreements which, despite variations of detail, obtain among them all in respect of this law.

Ibid., 1.11.11[3]

384. It has been shown that it was deficiency of human reasoning power that gave rise to a poetry so sublime that the philosophies that came afterward, the arts of poetry and criticism, have produced nothing equal and have even prevented its production . . . This discovery of the origins of poetry does away with the estimation of the matchless wisdom of the ancients, so ardently indulged in from Plato to Bacon's *De Sapientia Veterum*. For the wisdom of the ancients was the vulgar wisdom of the lawgivers who founded the human race, not the esoteric wisdom of the great and rare philosophers.

Ibid., 2.2.1[4]

Abstract sentences are the work of philosophers, because they contain universals, but reflections on the passions are the work of false and frigid poets.

PHILONOUS: I would first know whether I rightly understand your hypothesis. You make certain traces in the brain to be the causes or occasions of our ideas. Pray tell me, whether by the *brain* you mean any sensible thing?

HYLAS: What else think you I could mean?

PHILONOUS: Sensible things are all immediately perceivable; and those things which are immediately perceivable are ideas; and these exist only in the mind. Thus much you have, if I mistake not, long since agreed to.

HYLAS: I do not deny it.

PHILONOUS: **The brain therefore you speak of, being a sensible thing, exists only in the mind.** Now, I would fain know whether you think it reasonable to suppose, that one idea or thing existing in the mind, occasions all other ideas. And if you think so, pray how do you account for the origin of that primary idea or brain itself?

Three Dialogues Between Hylas and Philonous, 'The Second Dialogue'[1]

Some truths there are so near and obvious to the Mind, that a man need only open his eyes to see them. Such I take this important one to be, to wit, that all the Choir of Heaven and Furniture of the Earth, in a word, all those bodies which compose the mighty Frame of the World, have not any subsistence without a Mind, that their Being is to be perceived or known; that consequently so long as they are not actually perceived by me, or do not exist in my Mind or that of any other *created spirit*, they must either have no existence at all, *or else subsist in the Mind of some Eternal Spirit*: it being perfectly unintelligible and involving all the absurdity of Abstraction, to attribute to any single part of them an Existence independent of a spirit. To be convinced of which, the Reader need only reflect and try to separate in his own thoughts the being of a sensible thing from its being perceived.

A Treatise Concerning the Principles of Human Knowledge, 1.6[2]

PHILONOUS: That the colours are really in the tulip which I see, is manifest. Neither can it be denied, that this tulip may exist independent of your mind or mine; but that any immediate object of the senses, that is, any idea, or combination of ideas, should exist in an unthinking substance, is in itself an evident contradiction. Nor can I imagine how this follows from what you said just now, to wit that the red and yellow were on the tulip *you saw*, since you do not pretend to *see* that unthinking substance.

HYLAS: You have an artful way, Philonous, of diverting our inquiry from the subject.

Three Dialogues Between Hylas and Philonous, 'The First Dialogue'[3]

The brain therefore you speak of,
being a sensible thing, exists only
in the mind.

Some think that, nature having established paternal authority, the most natural government is that of a single person. But the example of paternal authority proves nothing. For if the power of the father relates to a single government, that of the brothers after the death of the father . . . refers to the government of the many . . . **Better it is to say that the government most conformable to nature is that which best agrees with the humour and disposition of the people in whose favour it is established.**

The Spirit of the Laws, 1.3, 'On Positive Laws'[1]

Law in general is human reason, inasmuch as it governs all the inhabitants of the earth: the political and civil laws of each nation ought to be only the particular cases in which human reason is applied.

They should be adapted in such a manner to the people for whom they are framed that it should be a remarkable coincidence if those of one nation should fit another . . .

They should be devised in relation to the climate of each country, to the quality of its soil, to its situation and size, to the principal occupations of its natives . . . to the degree of liberty the constitution will bear; to the religion of the inhabitants, to their inclinations, riches, numbers, commerce, manners and customs.

Ibid.[2]

True it is that when a democracy is founded on commerce, private people may acquire vast riches without a corruption of morals. This is because the spirit of commerce is naturally attended with that of frugality, economy, moderation, labour, prudence, tranquillity, order and rule. So long as this spirit subsists, the riches it produces have no bad effect. The mischief is, when excessive wealth destroys the spirit of commerce, then it is that the inconveniences of inequality begin to be felt.

In order to support this spirit, commerce should be carried out by the leading citizens; this should be their sole aim and study: this the chief object of the laws: and these very laws, by dividing the estates of the individuals in proportion to the increase of commerce, should set every poor citizen so far at his ease to be able to work like the rest, and every rich citizen in such a mediocrity as to be obliged to take new pains in either preserving or acquiring a fortune.

Ibid., 1.6, 'In What Manner the Laws Ought to Maintain Frugality in a Democracy'[3]

Better it is to say that the government most conformable to nature is that which best agrees with the humour and disposition of the people in whose favour it is established.

The horrible discord, which has lasted for so many centuries, is a most striking lesson that we should mutually forgive our errors. **Dissension is the great evil of mankind, and toleration its only remedy.**

There is nobody who does not agree with this truth, whether he meditates calmly in his study, or whether he peacefully examines the truth with his friends. Why, then, do the same men who in private approve forbearance, beneficence, justice, so vehemently denounce these virtues in public? Because self-interest is their god, because they sacrifice everything to this monster they worship.

Philosophical Dictionary, 'Toleration'[1]

It is clear that every individual who persecutes a man, his brother, because he does not agree with him is a monster.
Ibid.[2]

We know that every sect is a generator of error. There are no sects of geometricians, algebraists, arithmeticians because all the propositions of geometry, algebra and arithmetic are true.
Ibid.[3]

The greatest misfortune of a writer is not perhaps to be the object of his colleagues' jealousy, the victim of intrigue, to be despised by the powerful of the world – it is to be judged by fools. Fools sometimes go far, especially when ineptitude is added to fanaticism, and vengefulness to ineptitude. It is also a great misfortune of writers that they usually stand alone. A bourgeois buys a minor post and obtains with it the support of his colleagues. If he is the victim of an injustice, he at once has

defenders. The man of letters is helpless. He is like a flying fish: if he rises a little, the birds devour him, if he dives, he is fish-food.
Ibid., 'Literature and Writers'[4]

It is not inequality that is the real evil, but dependence.
Ibid., 'Equality'[5]

Enlighten men and you will be crushed.
Ibid., 'Literature and Writers'[6]

It's up to you to learn to think.
Ibid., 'Liberty of Thought'[7]

Dissension is the great evil of mankind, and toleration its only remedy.

But it is nevertheless true that the imagination alone perceives: it forms alone an idea of all objects, with the words and figures that characterize them; then, again, the imagination is the soul because it plays all the roles. **Thanks to the imagination, to its flattering touch, the cold skeleton of reason acquires living, rosy flesh; thanks to it the sciences flourish, the arts are embellished, woods speak, echoes sigh, rocks weep, marble breathes and all inanimate objects come to life** . . . It does not only follow in the train of the Graces and the fine arts; it does not only paint nature but can also measure her. It reasons, judges, penetrates, compares and analyses. Could it experience so acutely the beauty of the pictures that are drawn for it without understanding the relationships of their parts? No. In the same way as it cannot fall back on the senses without appreciating all their perfection or sensuality so it cannot reflect on what it has conceived mechanically without constituting judgement itself . . . It follows from the principles I have laid down that whoever has the most imagination has the most intellect or genius, because all these terms are synonyms.

Machine Man[1]

Imagination is true or false, strong or weak. True imagination represents objects in the natural state, while in false imagination the soul sees them as other than they are. Sometimes it recognizes this illusion and then it is only a vertigo like Pascal's, who had so exhausted his brain through study that he imagined he saw to his left an abyss of flame from which he always protected himself with chairs or any other kind of barrier which could shield from his view that terrifying, phantasmal chasm whose meaning was not lost on the great man. Sometimes the soul participates in the general error of all the internal and external senses and believes that the object in truth resembles the phantasms of the imagination and then it is true delirium.

Treatise on the Soul, 9, 'On Imagination'[2]

The weight of the universe, far from crushing the true atheist, does not even make him stagger.

Machine Man[3]

Man's first asset is his organization.

Ibid.[4]

Everything depends absolutely on the diversity of organization.

Ibid.[5]

Thanks to the imagination, to its flattering touch, the cold skeleton of reason acquires living, rosy flesh; thanks to it the sciences flourish, the arts are embellished, woods speak, echoes sigh, rocks weep, marble breathes and all inanimate objects come to life.

When I shall be dead, the principles of which I am composed will still perform their part in the universe and will be equally useful in the grand fabric, as when they composed this individual creature. The difference to the whole will be no greater than betwixt my being in my chamber and in the open air. The one change is of more importance to me than the other; but not more so to the universe.

'On Suicide'[1]

But the life of a man is of no greater importance to the universe than that of an oyster: and were it of ever so great importance, the order of human nature has actually submitted it to human prudence, and reduced us to a necessity, in every incident, of determining concerning it.

Ibid.[2]

A man who retires from life does no harm to society: he only ceases to do good; which, if it is an injury, is of the lowest kind.

Ibid.[3]

Were our horrors of annihilation an original passion, not the effect of our general love of happiness, it would rather prove the mortality of the soul: for as nature does nothing in vain, she would never give us a horror against an impossible event . . . Death is in the end unavoidable; yet the human species could not be preserved had not our nature inspired us with an aversion towards it.

'On the Immortality of the Soul'[4]

The identity, which we ascribe to the mind of man, is only a fictitious one, and of like kind with that which we ascribe to vegetables and animal bodies.

A Treatise of Human Nature, 1.4.6[5]

Identity depends on the relations of ideas; and these relations produce identity, by means of that easy transition they occasion. But as the relations, and the easiness of the transition may diminish by insensible degrees, we have no just standard, by which we can decide any dispute concerning the time, when they acquire or lose a title to the name of identity. All the disputes therefore concerning the identity of connected objects are merely verbal, except so far as the relation of the parts gives rise to some fiction, or imaginary principle of union . . .

Ibid.[6]

When I shall be dead, the
principles of which I am
composed will still perform their
part in the universe and will be
equally useful in the grand fabric,
as when they composed this
individual creature.

No matter of fact can be proved but from its cause or effect. Nothing can be known to be the cause of another but by experience. **We can give no reason for extending to the future our experience in the past; but are entirely determined by custom, when we conceive an effect to follow from its usual cause.** But we also believe an effect to follow as well as conceive it. This belief joins no new idea to the conception. It only varies the manner of conceiving, and makes a difference to the feeling or sentiment. Belief, therefore, in all matters of fact arises only from custom, and is an idea conceived in a particular *manner*.

A Treatise of Human Nature, Abstract[7]

Let men be once fully persuaded of these two principles, *That there is nothing in any object, consider'd in itself, which can afford us a reason for drawing a conclusion beyond it*; and *That even after the observation of the frequent or constant conjunction of objects, we have no reason to draw any inference concerning any object beyond those of which we have had experience*; I say let men be once fully convinc'd of these two principles, and this will throw them loose from all common systems, that they will make no difficulty of receiving any, which may appear the most extraordinary.

Ibid., 1.3.12[8]

We need only reflect on what has been prov'd at large, that we are never sensible of any connexion betwixt causes and effects, and that 'tis only by our experience of their constant conjunction, we can arrive at any knowledge of this relation.

Ibid., 1.4.4[9]

We can give no reason for
extending to the future our
experience in the past; but are
entirely determined by custom,
when we conceive an effect to
follow from its usual cause.

Man is born free; and everywhere he is in chains. One thinks himself the master of others, and still remains a greater slave than they. How did this change come about? I do not know. What can make it legitimate? That question I think I can answer.

If I took into account only force, and the effects derived from it, I should say: 'As long as a people is compelled to obey, and obeys, it does well; as soon as it can shake off the yoke, and shakes it off, it does still better; for, regaining its liberty by the same right as took it away, either it is justified in rescuing it, or there was no justification for those who took it away.' But the social order is a sacred right which is the basis of all other rights. Nevertheless, this right does not come from nature and must, therefore, be found in convention.

The Social Contract, 1.1[1]

One is free although subjected to laws, and not when one obeys a man, since in the latter case I am obeying the will of another, but when I obey the law I am only obeying the public will, which is mine as much as anyone else's.

Political Fragments, 4, 'On Laws'[2]

Freedom does not consist as much in acting according to one's own will as in not being subjected to the will of anyone else; it also consists in not subjecting the will of another to one's own. Whoever is master cannot be free, and to rule is to obey.

Letters Written from the Mountain, 8[3]

Thus the same causes that make us wicked also make us slaves, and our weakness arises from our cupidity. Our needs bring us together in proportion as our passions divide us, and the greater enemies we become, the less we can do without each other.

Political Fragments, 1, 'On the State of Nature'[4]

Besides, the right of property being only a convention of human institution, men may dispose of what they possess as they please: but this is not the case with the essential gifts of nature, such as life and liberty, which every man is permitted to enjoy, and of which it is at least doubtful whether any have the right to divest themselves. By giving up the one, we degrade our being; by giving up the other, we do our best to annul it; and as no temporal good can indemnify us for the loss of either, it would be an offence against both reason and nature to renounce them at any price whatsoever.

Discourse on the Origin of Inequality, 2[5]

The universal spirit of the laws of each and every country is to favour the strong against the weak and those who have against those who have not. This inconvenience is inevitable and it is without exception.

Émile, 4[6]

Laws and the practices of justice among us are only the art of sheltering the rich and powerful from the just reprisals of the poor.

Political Fragments, 4, 'On Laws'[7]

Man is born free; and everywhere he is in chains.

How did they meet? By chance, like everyone else. What were their names? What's that got to do with you? Where were they going to? **Does anyone really know where they're going to?** What were they saying? The master wasn't saying anything and Jacques was saying that his Captain used to say that everything which happens to us on this earth, both good and bad, is written up above.

MASTER: That's very profound.

JACQUES: My Captain used to add that every shot fired from a gun had someone's name on it.

MASTER: And he was right . . .

(*After a short pause* JACQUES *cried out:*) May the devil take that innkeeper and his inn.

Jacques the Fatalist and His Master[1]

Men have banished God from their midst. They have relegated him to a sanctuary. The walls of a temple circumscribe his life. It does not reach beyond.

Pensées Philosophiques, 26[2]

The true martyr waits for death; the fanatic chases after it.

Ibid., 39[3]

It's childhood education that forbids baptism to a Muslim; it's childhood education which forbids circumcision to a Christian; it's adult reason which scorns equally baptism and circumcision.

Additions aux Pensées Philosophiques, 33[4]

To say man is made up of strength and weakness, of light and blindness, of smallness and grandeur, is not to put him on trial – it's to define him.

Ibid., 41[5]

Old people all fear dying. Life isn't really disdained except by those who are assured of a long future. Since they do not know death, how can they attach importance or contempt to it? They live like all the others do, without thinking about it.

Essai sur les Règnes de Claude et de Néron, 'On Seneca's 58th Letter'[6]

Yesterday the wife betrayed the man she mourns today. Her grief shuts the door to his friends but not to her lover. The husband's corpse is in the vestibule, the adulterer is in the bed. A husband's dying day is marked with a solemn ceremony of hypocrisy.

Ibid., 'On Seneca's 63rd Letter'[7]

Does anyone really know where they're going to?

Imagine people waking from a deep sleep and, finding themselves in the middle of a labyrinth, proposing general principles for discovering the way out. What could be more ridiculous? Nevertheless, this is how philosophers behave. **We are born into the middle of a labyrinth where a thousand turns are laid out for the sole purpose of leading us astray.** If there is a way leading to truth, it is not at first apparent. Often it is the one that appears to least warrant our confidence. Thus we cannot be too cautious. Let us proceed slowly, examine carefully all the places we go through, and acquaint ourselves with them so thoroughly that we are able to retrace our steps. It is more important to find ourselves merely where we were at first than to believe prematurely that we are out of the labyrinth.

A Treatise on Systems, 2[1]

Abstract principles are not even a proper means for leading us to discoveries, for, as they are merely an abbreviated expression of our acquired knowledge, they can only take us back to this original knowledge. In short they are maxims containing what we already know. And as the common people have proverbs, these so-called principles are philosophers' proverbs and that is all they are.

Ibid.[2]

Consider enlightenment. As soon as we receive it we experience a new life and one that is indeed different from that which raw sensations . . . obtained for us in the past. Consider sentiment. Observe it especially where it is increased by all the judgements we are accustomed to confuse with sensory impressions.

Thereupon, these sensations, which presented at first only a few gross pleasures, will give birth to delicate pleasures which will succeed each other in astonishing variety. Thus the further we get from what our sensations were in the beginning, the more the life of our being develops and becomes variegated: it will come to embrace so many things that we will have difficulty in understanding how all our faculties could have a common principle in sensation.

A Treatise On the Sensations, 4.9[3]

We are born into the middle of a
labyrinth where a thousand turns
are laid out for the sole purpose
of leading us astray.

Our nature is so constituted that our *intuition* can never be other than sensible; that is, it contains only the mode in which we are affected by objects. The faculty, on the other hand, which enables us to *think* the object of sensible intuition is the understanding. To neither of these powers may a preference be given over the other. Without sensibility no object would be given to us, without understanding no object would be thought. **Thoughts without content are empty, intuitions without concepts are blind.** It is, therefore, just as necessary to make our concepts sensible, that is, to add the object to them in intuition, as to make our intuitions intelligible, that is, to bring them under concepts. These two powers or capacities cannot exchange their function. The understanding can intuit nothing, the senses can think nothing. Only through their union can knowledge arise.

Critique of Pure Reason, A51/B75[1]

What we have meant to say is that all our intuition is nothing but the representation of appearance; that the things which we intuit are not themselves what we intuit them as being, nor their relations so constituted in themselves as they appear to us, and that if the subject, or even only the subjective constitution of the senses in general, be removed, the whole constitution and all the relations of objects in space and time, nay space and time themselves, would vanish. As appearances, they cannot exist in themselves, but only in us. What objects may be in themselves, and apart from all this receptivity of our sensibility, remains completely unknown to us.

Ibid., A42/B59[2]

Now all experience does indeed contain, in addition to the intuition of the senses through which something is given, a *concept* of an object as being thereby given, that is to say, as appearing. Concepts of objects in general thus underlie all empirical knowledge as its *a priori* conditions. The objective validity of the categories as *a priori* concepts rests, therefore, on the fact that, so far as the form of thought is concerned, through them alone does experience become possible. They relate of necessity and *a priori* to objects of experience, for the reason that only by means of them can any object whatsoever of experience be thought.

Ibid., A93/B126[3]

Thoughts without content are
empty, intuitions without
concepts are blind.

Suppose, however, there was something *whose existence* has *in itself* an absolute value, something which as *an end in itself* could be a ground for determinate laws; then in it, and in it alone, would there be a ground of a possible categorical imperative – that is, of a practical law.

Now I say that man, and indeed every rational being, exists as an end in himself, not merely as a means for arbitrary use by this or that will: he must in all his actions, whether they are directed to himself or to other rational beings, always be viewed at the same time as an end . . .

The practical imperative will therefore be as follows: ***Act in such a way that you always treat humanity, whether in your own person or in the person of any other, never simply as a means, but always at the same time as an end.***

Groundwork of the Metaphysic of Morals, 64–6[4]

Finally, there is an imperative which, without being based on, and conditioned by, any further purpose to be attained by a certain line of conduct, enjoins that conduct immediately. This imperative is *categorical*. It is concerned, not with the action and its presumed results, but with its form and with the principle from which it follows; and what is essentially good in the action is the mental disposition, let the consequences be what they may. This imperative may be called the imperative of *morality*.

Ibid., 43[5]

There is . . . only a single categorical imperative and it is this: *Act only on that maxim through which you can at the same time will that it should become a universal law.*

Ibid., 52[6]

Everything good that is not based on a morally good disposition . . . is nothing but pretence and glittering misery.

Idea for a Universal History[7]

Two things fill the mind with ever new and increasing admiration and awe, the oftener and more steadily we reflect on them: the starry heavens above and the moral law within.

Critique of Practical Reason[8]

Act in such a way that you always treat humanity, whether in your own person or in the person of any other, never simply as a means, but always at the same time as an end.

Genius is the talent (or natural gift) that gives the rule to art. Since talent, as the innate productive faculty of the artist, belongs itself to nature, we may express the matter thus: *Genius* is the innate mental predisposition (*ingenium*) *through which* nature gives the rule to art.

126]   *Critique of Judgement*, 307[9]

(1) Genius is a talent for producing something for which no determinate rule can be given, not a mere aptitude for what can be learned by following some rule or other, hence its foremost property must be *originality*. (2) Since nonsense too can be original, the products of genius must also be models; i.e. they must be *exemplary*; hence, though they do not themselves arise through imitation, still they must serve others for this, i.e. as a standard or rule by which to judge. (3) Genius itself cannot describe or indicate scientifically how it brings about its products, and it is rather as *nature* that it gives the rule. That is why, if an author owes a product to his genius, he himself does not know how he came by his ideas for it; nor is it in his power to devise such products at his pleasure, or by following a plan, and to communicate [his procedure] to others in precepts that would enable them to bring about like products. (Indeed, that is presumably why the word genius is derived from [Latin] *genius*, [which means] the guardian and guiding spirit that each person is given as his own at birth, and to whose inspiration those original ideas are due.) (4) Nature, through genius, prescribes the rule not to science but to art, and this only insofar as the art is to be fine art.

Ibid.[10]

In scientific matters . . . the greatest discoverer differs from the most arduous imitator and apprentice only in degree, whereas he differs in kind from someone whom nature has endowed for fine art. But saying this does not disparage those great men to whom the human race owes so much in contrast to those whom nature has endowed for fine art. For the scientists' talent lies in continuing to increase the perfection of our cognitions and on all the dependent benefits, as well as on imparting that same knowledge to others; and in these respects they are far superior to those who merit the honour of being called geniuses. For the latter's art stops at some point, because a boundary is set for it beyond which it cannot go and which has probably long since been reached and cannot be extended further.

Ibid., 309[11]

Of all the arts *poetry* (which owes its origin almost entirely to genius and will least be guided by precept or examples) holds the highest rank.

Ibid., 326[12]

Genius is the talent (or natural gift)
that gives the rule to art.

Enlightenment is man's release from his self-incurred tutelage.
Tutelage is man's inability to make use of his understanding without direction from another. Self-incurred is this tutelage when its cause lies not in lack of reason but in lack of resolution or courage to use it without direction from another. *Sapere Aude!* 'Dare to reason for yourself!' – that is the motto of enlightenment.

What is Enlightenment?[13]

Since the philosopher cannot presuppose any [conscious] individual purpose among men in their great drama, there is no other expedient for him except to try to see if he can discover a natural purpose in this idiotic course of things human.

Idea for a Universal History[14]

A society in which freedom under external laws is associated in the highest degree with irresistible power, i.e. a perfectly just civic constitution, is the highest problem Nature assigns to the human race; for Nature can achieve her other purposes for mankind only upon the solution and completion of this assignment.

Ibid.[15]

Enlightenment comes gradually, with intermittent folly and caprice, as a great good which must finally save men from the selfish self-aggrandisement of their masters, always assuming they know their own interest. This enlightenment, and with it a certain commitment of the heart which the enlightened man cannot fail to make to the good he clearly understands, must step by step ascend the throne and influence the principles of government.

Ibid.[16]

That kings should philosophize or philosophers become kings is not to be expected. Nor is it to be wished, since the possession of power inevitably corrupts the untrammelled judgement of reason. But kings or king-like peoples which rule themselves under laws of equality should not suffer the class of philosophers to disappear or to be silent but should let them speak openly. This is indispensable to the enlightenment of the business of government, and, since the class of philosophers is by nature incapable of plotting and lobbying, it is above suspicion of being made up of propagandists.

Perpetual Peace[17]

Enlightenment is man's release from his self-incurred tutelage.

An intelligent child who is brought up with a mad child can go mad. **Man is so perfectible and corruptible that he can become a madman through sheer intellect.**

Aphorisms[1]

A man can never really know whether he isn't sitting in a madhouse.

Ibid.[2]

Everyone should study at least enough philosophy and *belles lettres* to make his sexual experience more delectable.

Ibid.[3]

If an angel were to tell us about his philosophy, I believe that many of his statements might well sound like $2 \times 2 = 13$.

Ibid.[4]

Instead of saying that the world is mirrored in us, we should rather say that our reason is mirrored in the world. We can do no other than to detect order and wise government in the world, but this follows from the structure of our minds. But it does not follow that something which we must necessarily think, is really so, for we have no concept whatsoever of the true character of the external world. Thus no proof of the existence of God is possible on this basis alone.

Ibid.[5]

The more experiences and experiments accumulate in the explanation of nature, the more precarious the theories become. But it is not always good to discard them immediately on this account. For every hypothesis which once was sound was useful for thinking of previous phenomena in the proper interrelations and for keeping them in context. We ought to set down contradictory experiences separately, until enough have accumulated to make building a new structure worthwhile.

Ibid.[6]

In nature we see not words but only the initial letters of words, and if we then try to read, we discover that the new so-called words are again only the initials of others.

Ibid.[7]

To read means to borrow; to create out of one's reading is paying off one's debts.

Ibid.[8]

Man is so perfectible and
corruptible that he can become a
madman through sheer intellect.

Publicity is the very soul of justice. It is the keenest spur to exertion, and the surest of guards against improbity. It keeps the Judge himself, while trying, under trial. Under the auspices of publicity, the cause in the court of law, and the appeal to the court of public opinion are going on at the same time. So many by-standers as an unrighteous Judge, or rather, a Judge who would otherwise be unrighteous, beholds attending in his court, so many witnesses he sees of his unrighteousness, so many condemning Judges, so many ready executioners, and so many industrious proclaimers of his sentence. By publicity the court of law, to which his judgement is appealed from, is secured against the want of evidence of his guilt. **It is through publicity alone that justice becomes the mother of security.**

Draught of a Code for the Organization of the Judicial Establishment in France[1]

A law may be defined as an assemblage of signs declarative of a volition conceived or adopted by the *sovereign* in a state, concerning the conduct to be observed in a certain *case* by a certain person or persons, who in the case in question are, or are supposed to be, subject to his power: such volition trusting for its accomplishment to the expectation of certain events which it is intended such declaration should on occasion be a means of bringing to pass, and the prospect of which it is intended should act as a motive upon those whose conduct is in question.

On Laws in General, 1.1[2]

Directly or indirectly, *well-being*, in one shape or another, or in several shapes, or all shapes taken together, is the subject of every thought, and the object of every action, on the part of every known *Being*, who is at the same time, a sensitive thinking being.

The Philosophy of Economic Science[3]

By the principle of utility is meant that principle which approves or disapproves of every action whatsoever, according to the tendency which it appears to have to augment or diminish the happiness of the party whose interest is in question: or, what is the same thing in other words, to promote or to oppose that happiness.

Introduction to the Principles of Morals and Legislation, 1.2[4]

The only common measure the nature of things affords is money.

Quoted in Elie Halévy, *La Formation du Radicalisme Philosophique*, Appendix 2[5]

It is through publicity alone that justice becomes the mother of security.

Attend to yourself: turn your attention away from everything that surrounds you and towards your inner life; this is the first demand that philosophy makes of its disciple. Our concern is not with anything that lies outside you, but only with yourself.

Science of Knowledge, First Introduction[1]

This intuiting of himself that is required of the philosopher in performing the act whereby the self arises for him, I refer to as intellectual intuition. It is the immediate consciousness that I act and of what I enact: it is that whereby I know something because I do it. We cannot prove from concepts that this power of intellectual intuition exists, nor deduce from them what it may be. Everyone must discover it immediately in himself, or he will never make its acquaintance.

... I cannot take a step, move a hand or foot, without an intellectual intuition of my self-consciousness accompanying these acts; only thus do I know that I do it, only thus do I distinguish my actions and myself therein from the object of action before me ... The source of life is contained therein, and without it there is death.

Ibid.[2]

According to the Science of Knowledge ... the ultimate ground of all reality for the self is a primordial interaction between the self and some other existence outside it, of which nothing more can be said except that it is utterly opposed to the self. In the course of this interaction, nothing is brought into the self, nothing alien is imported; everything that develops in the self ... develops solely from itself by its own laws. The self is merely set in motion by this opponent, in order that it may act; without such an external prime mover it would never have acted, and since its existence consists solely in acting, it would never have existed either.

Ibid.[3]

Attend to yourself: turn your attention away from everything that surrounds you and towards your inner life; this is the first demand that philosophy makes of its disciple.

[Men nowadays] do not seek what they need to supplement their own efforts towards self-development or the enrichment of their inner life. With respect to such ends, every association that one enters into, from the very earliest educational ties onwards, is a hindrance. At the very outset the youthful spirit, instead of enjoying free play and opportunity to see world and man as a whole, is retarded by alien and alienating ideas and early accustomed to a life of prolonged spiritual bondage. **In the midst of wealth, what lamentable poverty!**

Soliloquies, 3, 'The World'[1]

For now as never before may man justly boast of his mastery over the natural world. However much remains undone, enough has been accomplished to make him feel lord over the earth . . . [W]ith regard to this purpose I feel that communion with mankind augments my powers in every moment of my life. Each of us plies his own particular trade, completing the work of someone he never knew, or preparing the way for another who in turn will scarcely recognize how much he owes to him . . . all are as it were part of a great organism . . .

But even so I regard the whole sense of a common material progress to be of little value; it is not further gain in this direction that I desire for the world; it causes me mortal agony that this, an unholy waste of its holy powers, should be regarded as mankind's entire task.

Ibid.[2]

All who would belong to a better world must for the present pine in dismal servitude! Whatever spiritual association now exists is debased in service of the earthly. Aimed at some utility, it confines the spirit and does violence to the inner life.

Ibid.[3]

The sum total of religion is to feel that, in its highest unity, all that moves in us in feeling is one; to feel that any single and particular thing is only possible by means of this unity; to feel, that is to say, that our being and living is a being and living in and through God.

On Religion, 2, 'The Nature of Religion'[4]

In the midst of wealth, what lamentable poverty!

Philosophy . . . has to do, not with *unessential* determinations, but with a determination in so far as it is essential; its element and content is not the abstract or non-actual, but the *actual*, that which posits itself and is alive within itself – existence within its own Notion. It is the process which begets and traverses its own moments, and this whole movement constitutes what is positive and its truth. This truth therefore contains the negative also, what would be called the false, if it could be regarded as something from which one might abstract. The evanescent itself must, on the contrary, be regarded as essential, not as something fixed, cut off from the True and left lying who knows where outside it, any more than the True is to be regarded as something on the other side, positive and dead. Appearance is the arising and passing away that does not itself arise and pass away, but is 'in itself' [i.e. subsists intrinsically], and constitutes the actuality and the movement of the life of truth. **The True is thus the Bacchanalian revel in which no member is not drunk; yet because each member collapses as soon as he drops out, the revel is just as much transparent and simple repose.**

The Phenomenology of Spirit, Preface[1]

The True is the whole. But the whole is nothing other than the essence consummating itself through its development.

Ibid.[2]

What is rational is actual and what is actual is rational. On this conviction the plain man like the philosopher takes his stand, and from it philosophy starts in its study of the universe of mind as well as the universe of nature.

The Philosophy of Right, Preface[3]

Since the man of common sense makes his appeal to feeling, to an oracle within his breast, he is finished and done with anyone who does not agree; he has only to explain that he has nothing more to say to anyone who does not find and feel the same in himself. In other words, he tramples underfoot the roots of humanity. For it is the nature of humanity to press onward to agreement with others; human nature only really exists in an achieved community of minds. The anti-human, the merely animal, consists in staying within the sphere of feeling, and being able to communicate only at that level.

The Phenomenology of Spirit, Preface[4]

The True is thus the Bacchanalian revel in which no member is not drunk; yet because each member collapses as soon as he drops out, the revel is just as much transparent and simple repose.

And it is only through staking one's life that freedom is won; only thus is it proved that for self-consciousness, its essential consciousness is not [just] being, not the *immediate* form in which it appears, not its submergence in the expanse of life, but rather that there is nothing present in it which could not be regarded as a vanishing moment, that it is pure *being-for-self*. **The individual who has not risked his life may well be recognized as a *person*, but he has not attained to the truth of this recognition as an independent self-consciousness.**

The Phenomenology of Spirit, 'Lordship and Bondage'[5]

Self-consciousness exists in and for itself when, and by the fact that, it so exists for another; that is, it exists only in being acknowledged.

Ibid.[6]

Every self-consciousness knows itself (i) as universal, as the potentiality of abstracting from everything determinate, and (ii) as particular, with a determinate object, content and aim. Still, both these moments are only abstractions; what is concrete and true (and everything true is concrete) is not the universality which has the particular as its opposite, but the particular which by its reflection into itself has been equalized with the universal. This unity is individuality, not individuality in its immediacy as a unit, our first idea of individuality, but individuality in accordance with its concept; indeed, individuality in this sense is just precisely the concept itself.

The Philosophy of Right[7]

The individual who has not
risked his life may well be
recognized as a *person*, but he has
not attained to the truth of this
recognition as an independent
self-consciousness.

A fragment, like a miniature work of art, has to be entirely isolated from the surrounding world and be complete in itself like a porcupine.

Athenäum Fragments, 206[1]

Many of the works of the ancients have become fragments. Many modern works are fragments as soon as they are written.

Ibid., 24[2]

A: You say that fragments are the real form of universal philosophy. The form is irrelevant. But what can such fragments do and be for the greater and more serious concern of humanity, the perfection of human knowledge?
B: Nothing but a Lessingean salt against spiritual sloth, perhaps a cynical *lanx satura** in the style of old Lucilius or Horace, or even the *fermeata cognitionis*† for a critical philosophy, marginal glosses to the text of the age.

Ibid., 259[3]

Philosophy is a shared search for omniscience.

Ibid., 344[4]

As the finest flower of a particular kind of organization, poetry is a very localized thing. Philosophy, on the other hand, may possibly be not very dissimilar even on different planets.

Ideas, 75[5]

If you want to penetrate into the heart of physics, then let yourself be initiated into the mysteries of poetry.

Ibid., 99[6]

One shouldn't try to seduce or talk anyone into philosophy.

Athenäum Fragments, 417[7]

* A full plate or a rich satire
† Intellectual yeast

A fragment, like a miniature work of art, has to be entirely isolated from the surrounding world and be complete in itself like a porcupine.

The need to raise itself above humanity is humanity's main characteristic.

Ideas, 21[8]

Man is Nature creatively looking back on itself.

Ibid., 28[9]

The artist who doesn't reveal himself completely is a contemptible slave.

Ibid., 113[10]

An ideal is at once idea and fact. If ideals don't have as much individuality for the thinker as the gods of antiquity do for the artist, then any concern with ideas is no more than a boring and laborious game of dice with hollow phrases . . . Nothing is more wretched and contemptible than this sentimental speculation without any object. But one shouldn't call this mysticism, since this beautiful old word is so very useful and necessary for absolute philosophy, from whose perspective everything is a mystery and a wonder, while from other perspectives it would appear theoretically and practically normal.

Athenäum Fragments, 121[11]

If we would seize and comprehend the general outline of history, we must keep our eye steadily upon it; and must not let our attention get confused with details or seduced by objects immediately present. Judging from the feelings of the present, nothing nearly so concerns us as the issue of peace and war, and this is natural as, from a practical perspective, they are both affairs of the greatest importance . . . But it is otherwise in universal history, when this is conceived in a comprehensive and expansive spirit.

Then the remotest past, the highest antiquity, is as much entitled to our attention as the passing events of the day or the pressing concerns of our own time.

Philosophy of History[12]

The need to raise itself above
humanity is humanity's main
characteristic.

We see from the foregoing how much the objective nature of war makes it a calculation of probabilities; now there is only one single element still wanting to make it a game, and that element it certainly is not without: it is chance. **There is no human affair which stands so constantly and generally**

in close connection with chance as war . . . We see, therefore, how from the commencement, the absolute, the mathematical as it is called, nowhere finds any sure basis in the calculations in the Art of War; and that from the outset there is a play of possibilities, probabilities, good and bad luck, which spreads about with all the coarse and fine threads of its web, and makes war of all branches of human activity the most like a gambling game.

    On War, 1.20[1]

War is nothing but a duel on an extensive scale . . . War is therefore an act of violence intended to compel our opponent to fulfil our will . . . Violence, that is to say physical force (for there is no moral force without the conception of States and Law), is therefore the means; the compulsory submission of the enemy to our will is the ultimate object. In order to attain this object fully, the enemy must be disarmed, and disarmament becomes therefore the immediate object of hostilities in theory.

    Ibid., 1.2[2]

As the use of physical power to the utmost extent by no means excludes the cooperation of the intelligence, it follows that he who uses force unsparingly, without reference to the bloodshed involved, must obtain a superiority if his adversary uses less vigour in its application. The former then dictates

the law to the latter, and both proceed to extremities to which the only limitations are those imposed by the amount of counter-acting force on each side.

    Ibid., 1.3[3]

War is a mere continuation of policy by other means.

We see, therefore, that war is not merely a political act, but also a real political instrument, a continuation of political commerce, a carrying out of the same by other means . . . [T]he political view is the object, war is the means, and the means must always include the object in our conception.

    Ibid., 1.24[4]

There is no human affair which
stands so constantly and generally
in close connection with chance
as war.

The vanity of existence is revealed in the whole form existence assumes: in the infiniteness of time and space contrasted with the finiteness of the individual in both; in the fleeting present as the sole form in which actuality exists; in the contingency and relativity of all things; in continual becoming without being; in continual desire without satisfaction; in the continual frustration of striving in which life consists. *Time* and that *perishability* of all things existing in time that time itself brings about is simply the form under which the will to live, which as thing in itself is imperishable, reveals to itself the vanity of its striving. **Time is that by virtue of which everything becomes nothingness in our hands and loses all real value.**

On the Vanity of Existence[1]

Everyone connects the present with his own individuality, and imagines that all present becomes extinguished therewith; that past and future are then without a present. But just as on the globe everywhere is above, so the form of all life is the present; and to fear death because it robs us of the present is no wiser than to fear that we can slip down from the round globe on the top of which we are now fortunately standing. The form of the present is essential to the objectification of the will. As an extensionless point, it cuts time which extends infinitely in both directions, and stands firm and immovable, like an everlasting midday without a cool evening, just as the actual sun burns without intermission, while only apparently does it sink into the bosom of the night.

World as Will and Representation, 1.54[2]

The earth rolls on from day into night; the individual dies; but the sun itself burns without intermission, an eternal noon. Life is certain to the will-to-live; the form of life is endless present; it matters not how individuals, the phenomena of the Idea, arise and pass away in time like fleeting dreams. Therefore suicide appears to us to be a vain and hence foolish action.

Ibid.[3]

Man alone carries about with him in abstract concepts the certainty of his own death, yet this can frighten him only very rarely and at particular moments, when some occasion calls it to the imagination. Against the mighty voice of nature reflection can do little. In man, as in the animal that does not think, there prevails as a lasting state of mind the certainty, springing from innermost consciousness, that he is nature, the world itself. By virtue of this, no one is noticeably disturbed by the thought of certain and never-distant death, but everyone lives on as though he is bound to live for ever.

Ibid.[4]

Not the least of the torments which plague our existence is the constant pressure of time which never lets us so much as draw breath but pursues us all like a taskmaster with a whip. It ceases to plague only him it has delivered over to boredom.

On the Suffering of the World[5]

Time is that by virtue of which
everything becomes nothingness
in our hands and loses all real
value.

The progress of the individual mind is not only an illustration but an indirect evidence of that of the general mind. The point of departure of the individual and the race being the same, the phases of the mind of a man correspond to the epochs of the race. **Now, each of us is aware, if he looks back on his own history, that he was a theologian in his childhood, a metaphysician in his youth and a natural philosopher in his manhood.** All men who are up to their age can verify this for themselves.

Course in Positive Philosophy[1]

All good intellects have repeated since Bacon's time that there can be no real knowledge but that which is based on observed facts. This is incontestable, in our present advanced stage: but, if we look back to the primitive stage of human knowledge, we shall see that it must have been otherwise then. If it is true that every theory must be based on observed facts, it is equally true that facts cannot be observed without the guidance of some theory. Without such guidance our facts would be desultory and fruitless; we could not retain them: for the most part we could not even perceive them.

Ibid.[2]

The best minds are agreed that our European education, still essentially theological, metaphysical and literary, must be superseded by a positive training, conformable to our times and needs . . . [T]he present exclusive specialism in our pursuits, and the consequent isolation of the sciences, spoil our teaching. If any student desires to form an idea of natural philosophy as a whole, he is compelled to go through

each department where it is now taught, as if he were to be just an astronomer, only a chemist, with the result that . . . his training must remain very imperfect. And yet his goal demands that he should obtain general positive conceptions of all the classes of natural phenomena. It is such an aggregate of positive conceptions . . . which must henceforth be the permanent basis of all human societies.

Ibid.[3]

Love, then, is our principle; order our basis; and progress our end. Such . . . is the essential character of the system of life that positivism offers for the definite acceptance of society, a system that regulates the whole course of our private and public existence by bringing feeling, reason and activity into permanent harmony.

Ibid.[4]

Now, each of us is aware, if he
looks back on his own history,
that he was a theologian in his
childhood, a metaphysician in his
youth and a natural philosopher
in his manhood.

In this age, the mere example of non-conformity, the mere refusal to bend the knee to custom, is itself a service. Precisely because the tyranny of opinion is such as to make eccentricity a reproach, it is desirable, in order to break through that tyranny, that people should be eccentric. **Eccentricity has always abounded when and where strength of character has abounded; and the amount of eccentricity in a society has generally been proportional to the amount of genius, mental vigour, and moral courage it contained.** That so few now dare to be eccentric marks the chief danger of the time.

On Liberty[1]

Society can and does execute its own mandates: and if it issues wrong mandates instead of right, or any mandates at all in things with which it ought not to meddle, it practises a social tyranny more formidable than many kinds of political oppression, since, though not usually upheld by such extreme penalties, it leaves fewer means of escape, penetrating much more deeply into the details of life, and enslaving the soul itself. Protection, therefore, against the tyranny of the magistrate is not enough: there needs protection also against the tyranny of the prevailing opinion and feeling; against the tendency of society to impose, by other means than civil penalties, its own ideas and practices as rules of conduct on those who dissent from them . . .

Ibid.[2]

The object of this Essay is to assert one very simple principle . . . That principle is, that the sole end for which mankind are warranted, individually or collectively, in interfering with the liberty of action of any of their number, is self-protection. That the only purpose for which power can be rightfully exercised over any member of a civilized community, against his will, is to prevent harm to others. His own good, either physical or moral, is not a sufficient warrant.

Ibid.[3]

Our merely social intolerance kills no one, roots out no opinions, but induces men to disguise them, or to abstain from any active effort in their diffusion . . . [T]he price paid for this sort of intellectual pacification is the sacrifice of the entire moral courage of the human mind. A state of things in which a large portion of the most active and inquiring intellects find it advisable to keep the general principles and grounds of their convictions within their own breasts, and attempt, in what they address to the public, to fit as much as they can of their own conclusions to premises which they have internally renounced, cannot send forth the open, fearless characters, and logical, consistent intellects who once adorned the thinking world. The sort of men who can be looked for under it, are either mere conformers to commonplace, or time-servers for truth, whose arguments on all great subjects are meant for their hearers, and are not those which have convinced themselves.

Ibid.[4]

All silencing of discussion is an assumption of infallibility.

Ibid.[5]

Eccentricity has always abounded when and where strength of character has abounded; and the amount of eccentricity in a society has generally been proportional to the amount of genius, mental vigour, and moral courage it contained.

To be GOVERNED is to be watched, inspected, spied upon, directed, law-driven, numbered, regulated, enrolled, indoctrinated, preached at, controlled, checked, estimated, censured, commanded, by creatures who have neither the right nor the wisdom nor the virtue to do so. To be GOVERNED is to be at every operation, at every transaction, noted, registered, counted, taxed, stamped, measured, numbered, assessed, licensed, authorized, admonished, prevented, forbidden, reformed, corrected, punished. It is, under pretext of public utility, and in the name of general interest, to be placed under contribution, drilled, fleeced, exploited, monopolized, extorted from, squeezed, hoaxed, robbed; then, at the slightest resistance, the first word of complaint, to be repressed, fined, vilified, harassed, hunted down, abused, clubbed, disarmed, bound, choked, imprisoned, judged, condemned, shot, deported, sacrificed, sold, betrayed; and to crown all, mocked, ridiculed, derided, outraged, dishonoured. That is government; that is its justice; that is its morality.

General Idea of Revolution in the Nineteenth Century[1]

If I were asked to answer the following question: *What is slavery?* and I should answer in one word, *It is murder*, my meaning would be understood at once. No extended argument would be required to show that the power to take from a man his thought, his will, his personality, is a power of life and death and that to enslave a man is to kill him. Why, then, to this other question: *What is property?* may I not likewise answer, *It*

is theft, without the certainty of being misunderstood; the second proposition being no other than a transformation of the first?

Theory of Property, 1.1[2]

Yes: all men believe and repeat that equality of conditions is identical with equality of rights, that *property* and *theft* are synonymous terms, that every advantage accorded, or rather usurped, in the name of superior talent or service, is iniquity and extortion. All men in their hearts, I say, bear witness to these truths; they need only to be made to understand it.

Ibid., 1.2[3]

To be GOVERNED is to be watched, inspected, spied upon, directed, law-driven, numbered, regulated, enrolled, indoctrinated, preached at, controlled, checked, estimated, censured, commanded, by creatures who have neither the right nor the wisdom nor the virtue to do so.

Now, if a man could constantly balance on the tip of the moment of choice, if he could stop being a person, if in his inmost being he were only an empty thought, if personality meant no more than to be a goblin which, while going through the motions, remained nevertheless unchanged, if that was how it was, it would be foolish to say it might be too late for a man to choose, for in a deeper sense there could be no question of choice. **Choice itself is decisive for a personality's content; in choice personality immerses itself in what is chosen, and when it does not choose it wastes consumptively away.**

Either/Or, 2.2. 'Equilibrium between the Aesthetic and the Ethical in the Development of Personality'[1]

Just as an heir, even if he inherits all the world's treasures, does not own them before coming of age, even the richest personality is nothing before he has chosen himself, and on the other hand, even what might be called the poorest personality is everything when he has chosen himself; for the great thing is not to be this or that, but to be oneself; and every person can be that if he wants.

Ibid.[2]

In irony, the subject continuously wants to get outside the object, and he achieves this by realizing at every moment that the object has no reality. In doubt, the subject is an eyewitness to a war of conquest in which every phenomenon is destroyed, because the essence must continuously lie behind it. In irony, the subject is continuously retreating, taking every phenomenon out of its reality in order to save itself –

that is, in order to preserve itself in negative independence of everything.

The Concept of Irony[3]

In the world of the spirit, the only one who is excluded is the one who shuts himself out; in the world of the spirit all are invited, and therefore what is said about it can be said safely and undauntingly: if it pertains to one single individual it pertains to all.

Eighteen Upbuilding Discourses[4]

From the very start, everything that is good in a person is silent, and just as it is essentially God's nature to live in secret, so also the good in a person lives in secret.

Ibid.[5]

Choice itself is decisive for a personality's content; in choice personality immerses itself in what is chosen, and when it does not choose it wastes consumptively away.

When death is the greatest danger, one hopes for life. But when one learns to know the even more horrifying danger, one hopes for death. **When the danger is so great that death has become the hope, then despair is the hopelessness of not even being able to die.**

It is in this latter sense, then, that despair is the sickness unto death, this tormenting contradiction, this sickness in the self; eternally to die, to die and not to die, to die death itself.

The Sickness unto Death[6]

So much is spoken about wasting one's life. But the only life wasted is the life of one who so lived it, deceived by life's pleasures or its sorrows, that he never became decisively, eternally conscious of himself as spirit, as self, or, what is the same, never became aware – and gained in the deepest sense the impression – that there is a God there and that 'he', himself, his self, exists before this God, which infinite gain is never come by except through despair.

Ibid.[7]

In general, the urge for solitude is a sign that there is after all spirit in a person and the measure of what spirit there is. So little do chattering nonentities and socializers feel the need for solitude that, like love-birds, if left alone for an instant they promptly die. As the little child must be lulled to sleep, so these need the soothing hushaby of social life to be able to eat, drink, sleep, pray, fall in love, etc. It isn't only in the Middle Ages that people have been aware of this need for solitude, but also in antiquity there was respect for what it means; while in the never ending sociality of our own day one shrinks from solitude to the point of

not knowing to what use to put it except (oh! excellent epigram) the punishment of law-breakers. Yet it is true; in our own day it is indeed a crime to have spirit, so the fact that such people, the lovers of solitude, are put into the same category as criminals is just as it should be.

Ibid.[8]

What afflicts the adult is not so much the illusion of hope as, no doubt among other things, the grotesque illusion of looking down from some supposedly higher vantage-point, free from illusion, upon the illusions of the young.

Ibid.[9]

When the danger is so great that
death has become the hope, then
despair is the hopelessness of not
even being able to die.

We set out from real, active men, and on the basis of their real life-process we demonstrate the development of the ideological reflexes and echoes of this life-process. The phantoms formed in the human brain are also, necessarily, sublimates of their material life-process, which is empirically verifiable and bound to material premises. Morality, religion, metaphysics, all the rest of ideology and their corresponding forms of consciousness, thus no longer retain the semblance of independence. They have no history, no development; but men, developing their material production and their mental intercourse, alter, along with their real existence, their thinking and the products of their thinking. **Life is not determined by consciousness, but consciousness by life.**

The German Ideology, 'The Materialist Conception of History'[1]

This crystallization of social activity, this consolidation of what we ourselves produce into an objective power above us, growing out of our control, thwarting our expectations, bringing to naught our calculations, is one of the chief factors in historical development up till now . . . This 'alienation' . . . can only be abolished given two practical premises. For it to become an 'intolerable' power, i.e. a power against which men make a revolution, it must necessarily have rendered the great mass of humanity 'propertyless' and produced, at the same time, the contradiction of an existing world of wealth and culture . . . And, on the other hand, this development of productive forces (which itself implies the actual existence of men in their *world-historical*, instead of local, being) is absolutely necessary as a practical premise . . . because only with this universal development of productive forces is a universal intercourse between men established, which produces in all nations simultaneously the phenomenon of the 'propertyless' mass (universal competition), makes each nation dependent on the revolutions of the others, and finally has put *world-historical*, empirically universal individuals in place of local ones . . . [T]he proletariat can thus only exist world-historically, just as communism, its movement, can only have a 'world-historical' existence.

Ibid., 'Consciousness and the Division of Labour'[2]

The history of all hitherto existing societies is the history of class struggles.

The Communist Manifesto[3]

Communism deprives no man of the power to appropriate the products of society; all that it does is to deprive him of the power to subjugate the labour of others by means of such an appropriation.

Ibid.[4]

Life is not determined by consciousness, but consciousness by life.

***One thing is needful*: To 'give style' to one's character – a great and rare art!** It is practised by those who survey all the strengths and weaknesses of their nature and then fit them into an artistic plan until every one of them appears as art and reason and even weaknesses delight the eye . . . In the end, when the work is finished, it becomes evident how the constraint of a single taste governed and formed everything large and small. Whether this taste was good or bad is less important than one might suppose, if only it was a single taste!

. . . For one thing is needful: that a human being should *attain* satisfaction with himself, whether it be by means of this or that poetry or art; only then is a human being at all tolerable to behold.

The Gay Science, 290[1]

Here it becomes necessary to take a bold running start and leap into the metaphysics of art, by repeating the sentence . . . that existence and the world seem justified only as an aesthetic phenomenon. In this sense, it is precisely the tragic myth that has to convince us that even the ugly and disharmonic are part of the artistic game that the will in the eternal amplitude of its pleasure plays with itself. But this primordial phenomenon of Dionysian art is difficult to grasp, and there is only one direct way to make it intelligible and grasp it immediately: through the wonderful significance of *musical dissonance*. Quite generally, only music, placed beside the world, can give us an idea of what is meant by the justification of the world as an aesthetic phenomenon. The joy aroused by the tragic myth has the same origin as the joyous sensation of dissonance in music. The Dionysian, with its primordial joy experienced even in pain, is the common source of music and tragic myth.

The Birth of Tragedy, 24[2]

Our ultimate gratitude to art: – If we had not welcomed the arts and invented this kind of cult of the untrue, then the realization of general untruth and mendaciousness that now comes to us through science – the realization that delusion and error are conditions of human knowledge and sensation – would be utterly unbearable. *Honesty* would lead to nausea and suicide. But now there is a counterforce against our honesty that helps to avoid such consequences: art as the *good* will to appearance.

The Gay Science, 107[3]

What a man *is* begins to betray itself when his talent decreases – when he stops showing what he *can* do. Talent, too, is finery; finery, too, is a hiding place.

Beyond Good and Evil, 'Epigrams and Interludes', 130[4]

One thing is needful: To 'give style' to one's character – a great and rare art!

The madman jumped into their midst and pierced them with his eyes. 'Whither is God?' he cried; 'I will tell you. *We have killed him* – you and I. All of us are his murderers. But how did we do this? How could we drink up the sea? Who gave us the sponge to wipe away the whole horizon? What were we doing when we unchained this earth from its sun? Whither is it moving now? Away from all suns? . . . Do we not need to light lanterns in the morning? Do we hear nothing yet of the gravediggers who are burying God? Do we smell nothing yet of the divine decomposition? Gods, too, decompose. **God is dead.** God remains dead. And we have killed him . . .'

The Gay Science, 125[5]

The entire history of ethnic struggle, victory, reconciliation, fusion, everything that precedes the definitive ordering of rank of the different national elements in every great racial synthesis, is reflected in the confused genealogies of their gods, in the sagas of the gods' struggles, victories, and reconciliations; the advance towards universal empires is always also an advance towards universal divinities; despotism with its triumph over the independent nobility always prepares the way for some kind of monotheism.

The Genealogy of Morals, 2.21[6]

It is the profound, suspicious fear of an incurable pessimism that forces whole millennia to bury their teeth in and cling to a religious interpretation of existence: the fear of that instinct which senses that one might get a hold of truth *too soon*, before man has become strong enough, hard enough, artist enough.

Beyond Good and Evil, 59[7]

Extreme positions are not succeeded by moderate ones but by extreme positions of the opposite kind. Thus the belief in the absolute of nature, in aim- and meaninglessness, is the psychologically necessary affect once the belief in God and an essentially moral order becomes untenable. Nihilism appears at that point, not that the displeasure at existence has become greater than before but because one has come to distrust any 'meaning' in suffering, indeed in existence. One interpretation has collapsed; but because it was considered *the* interpretation it now seems as if there were no meaning at all in existence, as if everything were in vain.

The Will to Power, Book 1: European Nihilism[8]

The 'real world' – an idea no longer of any use, not even a duty any longer – an idea grown useless, superfluous, *consequently* a refuted idea: let us abolish it!

(Broad daylight; breakfast, return of cheerfulness and *bon sens*; Plato blushes for shame; all free spirits run riot.)

We have abolished the real world: what world is left? the apparent world perhaps? . . . But no! *with the real world we have also abolished the apparent world!*

(Midday; moment of the shortest shadow; end of the longest error; zenith of mankind; INCIPIT ZARATHUSTRA [Zarathustra arises].)

Twilight of the Idols, 'How the "Real World" at Last Became a Myth'[9]

God is dead.

And do you know what 'the world' is to me? Shall I show it to you in my mirror? **This world: a monster of energy, without beginning, without end; a firm, iron magnitude of force that does not grow bigger or smaller, that does not expend itself but only transforms itself; as a whole, of unalterable size, a household without expenses or losses, but likewise without increase or income; enclosed by 'nothingness' as by a boundary; not something blurry or wasted, not something endlessly extended, but set in a definite space as a definite force, and not a space that might be 'empty' here or there, but rather as a force throughout, as a play of forces and waves of forces, at the same time one and many, increasing here and at the same time decreasing there; a sea of forces flowing and rushing and rushing together, eternally changing, eternally flooding back, with tremendous years of recurrence, with an ebb and a flood of its forms; out of the stillest, most rigid, coldest forms toward the hottest, most turbulent, most self-contradictory, and then again returning home to the simple out of this abundance, out of the play of contradictions back to the joy of concord, still affirming itself in this uniformity of its courses and its years, blessing itself as that which must return eternally, as a becoming that knows no satiety, no disgust, no weariness: this, my Dionysian world of the eternally self-destroying, this mystery world of the twofold voluptuous delight, my 'beloved good and evil', without goal, unless the joy of the circle is itself a goal; without will, unless a ring feels good will toward itself – do you want a *name* for this world? A** *solution* for all its riddles? A *light* for you, too, you best-concealed, strongest, most intrepid, most midnightly men? – *This world is the will to power – and nothing besides!* And you yourselves are also this will to power – and nothing besides!

The Will to Power, 1067[10]

I tell you: one must have chaos in one, to give birth to a dancing star. I tell you: you still have chaos in you.

Alas! The time is coming when man will give birth to no more stars.

Thus Spake Zarathustra, Prologue[11]

This world: a monster of energy, without beginning,
without end; a firm, iron magnitude of force that does
not grow bigger or smaller, that does not expend itself
but only transforms itself; as a whole, of unalterable size,
a household without expenses or losses, but likewise
without increase or income; enclosed by 'nothingness' as
by a boundary; not something blurry or wasted, not
something endlessly extended, but set in a definite space
as a definite force, and not a space that might be 'empty'
here or there, but rather as a force throughout, as a play
of forces and waves of forces, at the same time one and
many, increasing here and at the same time decreasing
there; a sea of forces flowing and rushing and rushing
together, eternally changing, eternally flooding back,
with tremendous years of recurrence, with an ebb and a
flood of its forms; out of the stillest, most rigid, coldest
forms toward the hottest, most turbulent, most self-
contradictory, and then again returning home to the
simple out of this abundance, out of the play of
contradictions back to the joy of concord, still affirming
itself in this uniformity of its courses and its years,
blessing itself as that which must return eternally, as a
becoming that knows no satiety, no disgust, no
weariness: this, my Dionysian world of the eternally self-
destroying, this mystery world of the twofold voluptuous
delight, my 'beloved good and evil', without goal, unless
the joy of the circle is itself a goal; without will, unless a
ring feels good will toward itself – do you want a *name*
for this world?

The Role of Experiment and Generalization – **Experiment is the sole source of truth.** It alone can teach us something new; it alone can give us certainty. These are two points that cannot be questioned.

Science and Hypothesis, 4.9[1]

The man of science must work with method. Science is built up of facts as a house is built of stones, but an accumulation of facts is no more a science than a heap of stones is a house.

Ibid.[2]

What then is a good experiment? It is that which teaches us something more than an isolated fact. It is that which enables us to predict and to generalize. Without generalization, prediction is impossible. The circumstances under which one has operated will never again be repeated simultaneously. The fact observed will never be repeated. All that can be affirmed is that under analogous circumstances an analogous fact will be produced.

Ibid.[3]

It is said that experiments should be made without preconceived ideas. That is impossible. Not only would it make experiment fruitless, but even if one wished to do so, it could not be done. Every man has his own conception of the world and this he cannot so easily lay aside. We must, for example, use language, and our language is necessarily steeped in preconceived ideas. Only they are unconscious preconceived ideas, which are a thousand times more dangerous.

Ibid.[4]

Every experiment must enable us to make a maximum of predictions having the highest degree of probability.

Ibid.[5]

It might be asked why in physical science generalization so readily takes the mathematical form . . . It is not only because we have to express numerical laws; it is because the observable phenomenon is due to the superimposition of a large number of elementary phenomena which are all similar to each other; and in this way, differential equations are quite naturally introduced. It is not enough that each elementary phenomenon should obey simple laws: all those that have to combine must obey the same law; only then is the intervention of mathematics of any use. Mathematics teaches us, in fact, to combine like with like. Its object is to divine the result of a combination without having to reconstruct that combination element by element.

Ibid.[6]

Experiment is the sole source of truth.

Only that which is essentially related to an other, each related element having its own proper essence, and on the same lines as the other, can in a true sense be said to form a connection with that other or build up a whole with it. Both immanent and absolute Being and transcendent Being are indeed 'being' and 'object', and each has, moreover, its objective, determining content, but it is evident that what then on either side goes by the name of object and objective determination bears the same name only when we speak in terms of empty logical categories. **Between the meanings of consciousness and reality there yawns a veritable abyss.** The latter is a Being which manifests itself perspectively, never giving itself absolutely, merely contingent and relative; the former is a necessary and absolute Being, fundamentally incapable of being given through appearance and perspective-patterns.

Ideas: A General Introduction to Pure Phenomenology[1]

Reality, that of the thing taken singly as also that of the whole world, essentially lacks independence . . . Reality is not in itself something absolute, binding itself to another only in a secondary way; it is, absolutely speaking, nothing at all; it has no 'absolute essence' whatsoever; it has the essentiality of something which in principle is *only* intuited, *only* known, i.e. consciously presented in appearance.

Ibid.[2]

We must always bear in mind that *what things are* (the things about which alone we can ever speak and concerning whose being or non-being, so being or not so being, we can alone contend or reach rational decisions), *they are as things of experience.* Experience alone prescribes their meaning, and indeed, when we are dealing with things that are founded on fact, it is actual experience in its definitively ordered empirical connections which does the prescribing . . . An object that has being in itself is never such as to be out of relation to consciousness and its Ego.

Ibid.[3]

Imperturbably I must hold fast to the insight that every sense that any existent whatever has or can have for me – in respect of its 'what' and its 'it exists and actually is' – is a sense *in* and *arising from* my intentional life, becoming clarified and uncovered for me in consequence of my life's constitutive syntheses, in systems of harmonious verification.

Cartesian Meditations, 5[4]

Between the meanings of consciousness and reality there yawns a veritable abyss.

Two views of the history of thought are usually proffered as irreconcilable opposites. According to one, it is the record of the most profound dealings of the reason with ultimate being; according to the other, it is a source of pretentious claims and ridiculous failures. Nevertheless, there is a point of view from which there is something common to the two notions, and this common denominator is more significant than the oppositions. **Meaning is wider in scope as well as more precious in value than truth, and philosophy is occupied with meaning rather than truth.** Making such a statement is dangerous; it is easily misconceived to signify that truth is of no great importance under any circumstances; while the fact is that truth is so infinitely important when it is important at all, namely, in regards of events and descriptions of existences, that we extend its claims to regions where it has no jurisdiction. But even as respects truths, meaning is the wider category; truths are but one class of meanings, namely, those in which a claim to verifiability by their consequences is an intrinsic part of the meaning. Beyond this island of meanings, which in their own nature are true or false, lies the ocean of meanings to which truth and falsity are irrelevant. We do not inquire whether Greek civilization was true or false, but we are immensely concerned to penetrate its meaning.

Philosophy and Civilization, Introduction[1]

It has become a cheap intellectual pastime to contrast the infinitesimal pettiness of man with the vastnesses of the stellar universes. Yet all such comparisons are illicit. We cannot compare existence and meaning; they are disparate. The characteristic life of a man is itself the meaning of vast stretches of existences, and without it the latter have no value or significance. There is no common measure of physical existence and conscious experience because the latter is the only measure there is of the former. The significance of being, though not its existence, is the emotion it stirs, the thought it sustains.

Ibid.[2]

Refusal to accept responsibility for looking ahead and for planning in matters national and international is based upon refusal to employ in social affairs, in the field of human relations, the methods of observation, interpretation and test that are matters of course in dealing with physical things, and to which we owe the conquest of physical nature. The net result is a state of imbalance, of profoundly disturbed equilibrium between our physical knowledge and our social-moral knowledge. This lack of harmony is a powerful factor in producing the present crisis with all its tragic features . . . [O]ur failure to use in matters of direct human concern the scientific methods which have revolutionized physical knowledge has permitted the latter to dominate the social scene.

The Democratic Faith and Education[3]

Meaning is wider in scope as well as more precious in value than truth, and philosophy is occupied with meaning rather than truth.

It would, I suppose, be universally admitted that time involves change. In ordinary language, indeed, we say that something can remain unchanged through time. But there could be no time if nothing changed. And if anything changes, then all other things change with it. For its change must change some of their relations to it, and so their relational properties. **The fall of a sandcastle on the English coast changes the nature of the Great Pyramid.**

The Nature of Existence, 2.5.33[1]

Take any event – the death of Queen Anne, for example – and consider what changes can take place in its characteristics. That it is a death, that it is the death of Anne Stuart, that it has such causes, that it has such effects – every characteristic of this sort never changes . . . At the last moment of time – if time has a last moment – it will still be the death of a Queen. And in every respect but one it is equally devoid of change. But in one respect it does change. It was once an event in the far future. It became every moment an event in the nearer future. At last it was present. Then it became past, and will always remain past, though every moment it becomes further and further past.

Ibid.[2]

If anything is to be rightly called past, present or future, it must be because it is in relation to something else. And this something else to which it is in relation must be something outside the time-series. For the relations of the A-series [past–present–future] are changing relations, and no relations which are exclusively between members of the time-series can ever change. Two events are in exactly the same place in the time-series, relatively to one another, a million years before they take place, while each of them is taking place and when they are a million years in the past.

Ibid.[3]

The reality of the A-series, then, leads to contradictions and must be rejected. And, since we have seen that change and time require the A-series, the reality of change and time must be rejected . . . Nothing is really past, present or future. Nothing is really earlier or later or temporally simultaneous with it. Nothing really changes. And nothing is really in time. Whenever we perceive anything in time – which is the only way in which, in our present experience, we do perceive things – we are perceiving it more or less as it really is not.

Ibid.[4]

The fall of a sandcastle on the
English coast changes the nature
of the Great Pyramid.

I cannot . . . prove that my view of the good life is right; I can only state my view, and hope that as many as possible will agree. My view is this:

The good life is one inspired by love and guided by knowledge.

Knowledge and love are both indefinitely extensible; therefore, however good a life may be, a better life may be imagined. Neither love without knowledge, nor knowledge without love can produce a good life.

'What I Believe'[1]

The purpose of the moralist is to improve men's behaviour. This is a laudable ambition, since their behaviour is for the most part deplorable. But I cannot praise the moralist either for the particular improvements he desires or for the methods he adopts for achieving them. His ostensible method is moral exhortation; his real method (if he is orthodox) is a system of economic rewards and punishments.

Ibid.[2]

There is no short cut to the good life, whether individual or social. To build up the good life, we must build up intelligence, self-control and sympathy. This is a quantitative matter, a matter of gradual improvement, of early training, of educational experiment. Only impatience prompts the belief in the possibility of sudden improvement.

Ibid.[3]

In the welter of competing fanaticisms, one of the few unifying forces is scientific truthfulness, by which I mean the habit of basing our beliefs upon observations and inferences as impersonal, and as much divested of local and temperamental bias, as is possible for human beings. To have insisted upon the introduction of this virtue into philosophy, and to have invented a powerful method by which it can be rendered fruitful, are the chief merits of the philosophical school of which I am a member [the school of logical analysis]. The habit of careful veracity acquired in the practice of this philosophical method can be extended to the whole sphere of human activity, producing, wherever it exists, a lessening of fanaticism with an increasing capacity of sympathy and mutual understanding. In abandoning part of its dogmatic pretensions, philosophy does not cease to suggest and inspire a way of life.

History of Western Philosophy, 31, 'The Philosophy of Logical Analysis'[4]

The good life is one inspired by love and guided by knowledge.

We are like sailors who must rebuild their ship on the open sea, never able to dismantle it in dry-dock and to reconstruct it out of the best materials. Only the metaphysical elements can be allowed to vanish without trace. Vague linguistic conglomerations remain in one way or another as components of the ship. If vagueness is diminished at one point, it may well be increased at another.

'Protocol Sentences'[1]

What is originally given to us is our *ordinary natural language* with a stock of imprecise, unanalysed terms. We start by purifying this language of metaphysical elements and so reach the *physicalistic ordinary language* . . . We believe that every word of the physicalistic ordinary language will prove to be replaceable by terms taken from the language of advanced science, just as one may also formulate the terms of the language of advanced science with the help of the terms of ordinary language . . . Einstein's theories are expressible (somehow) in the language of the Bantus – but not those of Heidegger, unless linguistic abuses to which the German language lends itself are introduced into Bantu. A physicist must, in principle, be able to satisfy the demand of the talented writer who insisted that: 'One ought to be able to make the outlines of any rigorously scientific thesis comprehensible to a hackney-coach-driver.'

Ibid.[2]

We are like sailors who must
rebuild their ship on the open
sea, never able to dismantle it in
dry-dock and to reconstruct it out
of the best materials.

On the question of the world as a whole, science founders. For scientific knowledge the world lies in fragments, the more so, the more precise our scientific knowledge becomes.

Liberation from obsolete world-views leads to misconceived science, to a new, supposedly scientific world-view which stifles our freedom more than any previous world-view has ever done.

Philosophy is for Everyman[1]

The trouble begins when the scientifically known is taken for Being itself, when everything not scientifically knowable is declared unexistent. Science then becomes scientific superstition, a heap of nonsense in the garb of pseudo-science, containing neither science nor philosophy nor faith.

Ibid.[2]

The world cannot be grasped as itself, nor as matter, nor as life, nor as mind. An unknowable reality precedes the knowable and is not attainable by knowledge. For our way of knowing, the world is unfathomable.

Ibid.[3]

The real world is appearance, not reality as such. We are thrown into this real world, where we orientate ourselves with the aid of valid scientific knowledge, but do not look beyond it. Only philosophical insight frees us from our imprisonment in this world.

Ibid.[4]

Man imprisoned in his empirical existence wants to transcend himself. Enclosed in himself and at rest, he finds no satisfaction in being nothing beyond the daily round of existence. He no longer knows himself authentically as man if he is content to be the man he is now.

Ibid.[5]

The vital consciousness of our empirical existence is not the same as the existential consciousness of our self. Only when life is shaken by the thought of death has *Existenz* awakened. *Existenz* either loses itself in despair in the face of nothingness or is given to itself in the certainty of eternity.

Real life in the world is either permeated with this awareness of eternity or it is futile.

Ibid.[6]

Philosophy addresses itself to individuals. It creates a free community of those who rely on each other in their will for truth. Into this community the philosopher would like to enter. It is there in the world at any time, but cannot become a worldly institution without losing the freedom of its truth. He cannot know whether he belongs to it. No authority decides on his acceptance. He wants to live in his thinking in such a way as to make his acceptance possible.

Ibid.[7]

On the question of the world as a
whole, science founders.

Thinking accomplishes the relation of Being to the essence of man. It does not make or cause the relation. Thinking brings this relation to being solely as something handed over to it from Being. Such offering consists in the fact that in thinking Being comes to language. **Language is the house of Being.** In its home man dwells. Those who think and those who create with words are the guardians of his home.

Letter on Humanism[1]

Language is the lighting-concealing advent of Being itself.

Ibid.[2]

Being is the nearest. Yet the near remains furthest from man. Man at first clings always and only to beings. But when thinking represents beings as beings it no doubt relates to Being. In truth, however, it always thinks only of beings as such; precisely not, and never, Being as such.

Ibid.[3]

Homelessness . . . consists in the abandonment of Being by beings. Homelessness is the symptom of oblivion of Being. Because of it the truth of being remains unthought. The oblivion of Being makes itself known indirectly through the fact that man always observes and handles only beings . . . Homelessness is coming to be the destiny of the world.

Ibid.[4]

JAPANESE: What you suggest confirms a surmise I have long cherished. Your phrase 'house of Being' must not be taken as a mere hasty image which helps us in imagining what we will, such as: a house is a shelter erected earlier somewhere or other, in which Being, like a portable object, can be stored away.

INQUIRER: That notion proves invalid as soon as we think of the ambiguity of 'Being' of which we have spoken. With that expression, I do not mean the Being of beings represented metaphysically, but the presence of Being, more precisely the presence of the two-fold, Being and beings – but this two-fold understood in respect of its importance for thinking them.

JAPANESE: If we heed this, then your phrase can never become a mere catchword.

INQUIRER: It already has become one.

'A Dialogue on Language'[5]

Language speaks.

Man speaks in that he responds to language. This responding is a hearing. It hears because it listens to the command of stillness.

'Language'[6]

Language is the house of Being.

Language sets everyone the same traps; it is an immense network of wrong turnings. And so we watch one man after another walking down the same paths and we know in advance where he will branch off, where walk straight on without noticing the side turning, etc. etc. What I have to do then is erect signposts at all the junctions where there are wrong turnings so as to help people past the danger points.

Miscellaneous Remarks on Culture and Value[1]

5.6   *The limits of my language* mean the limits of my world.

5.61   Logic fills the world: the limits of the world are also its limits.

   We cannot therefore say in logic: This and this there is in the world, that there is not.

   For that would apparently presuppose that we exclude certain possibilities, and this cannot be the case since otherwise logic must get outside the limits of the world: that is, if it could consider these limits from the other side also.

   What we cannot think, that we cannot think: we cannot therefore say what we cannot think.

Tractatus Logico-Philosophicus[2]

4.003   Most propositions and questions, that have been written about philosophical matters, are not false, but senseless. We cannot, therefore, answer questions of this kind at all, but only state their senselessness. Most questions and propositions of the philosophers result from the fact that we do not understand the logic of our language.

   Ibid.[3]

4.116   Everything that can be thought at all can be thought clearly. Everything that can be said can be said clearly.

   Ibid.[4]

4.121   Propositions cannot represent the logical form: this mirrors itself in the language.

   That which mirrors itself in language, language cannot represent.

   That which expresses *itself* in language, *we* cannot express by language.

   The propositions *show* the logical form of reality.

   They exhibit it.

   Ibid.[5]

7   Whereof one cannot speak, thereof one must be silent.

   Ibid.[6]

Sometimes a sentence can be understood only if it is read at the right *tempo*. My sentences are all supposed to be read slowly.

Miscellaneous Remarks on Culture and Value[7]

Language sets everyone the same traps; it is an immense network of wrong turnings.

In this way I should like to say the words 'Oh, *let* him come!' are charged with my desire. And words can be wrung from us, – like a cry. Words can be *hard to say*: such, for example, as are used to effect a renunciation, or to confess a weakness. (**Words are also deeds.**)

Philosophical Investigations, 546[8]

We are under the illusion that what is peculiar, profound, essential, in our investigation, resides in its trying to grasp the incomparable essence of language. That is, the order existing between the concepts of proposition, word, proof, truth, experience and so on. This order is a *super*-order between – so to speak – *super*-concepts. Whereas, of course, if the words 'language', 'experience', 'world', have a use, it must be as humble a one as that of the words 'table', 'lamp', 'door'.
98. On the other hand it is clear that every sentence in our language 'is in order as it is'. That is to say, we are not *striving after* an ideal, as if our ordinary vague sentences had not yet got a quite unexceptional sense, and a perfect language awaited construction by us. – On the other hand it seems clear that where there is sense there must be perfect order. – So there must be perfect order in the vaguest sentence.

Ibid., 97–8[9]

But how many kinds of sentence are there? Say assertion, question and command? – there are *countless* kinds: countless different kinds of use of what we call 'symbols', 'words', 'sentences'. And this multiplicity is not something fixed, given once and for all; but new types of language, new language-games, as we may say, come into existence, and others become obsolete and get forgotten. (we can get a *rough picture* of this from the changes in mathematics.)

Hence the term 'language-*game*' is meant to bring into prominence the fact that the *speaking* of language is part of an activity, or a form of life.

Ibid., 23[10]

The question 'What is a word really?' is analogous to 'What is a piece in chess?'
Ibid., 108[11]

No one *can* speak the truth; if he still has not mastered himself. He *cannot* speak it; – but not because he is not clever enough yet.

The truth can be spoken only by someone who is already *at home* in it; not by someone who still lives in falsehood and reaches out from falsehood towards truth on just one occasion.

Miscellaneous Remarks on Culture and Value[12]

Words are also deeds.

There is no more light in a genius than in any other honest man – but he has a particular kind of lens to concentrate this light into a burning point.

Miscellaneous Remarks on Culture and Value[13]

Working in philosophy – like work in architecture in many respects – is really more a working on oneself. On one's own interpretations. On one's way of seeing things. (And of what one expects of them.)

Ibid.[14]

A philosopher easily gets into the position of an incompetent manager who instead of getting on with his *own* work and just keeping an eye on his employees to make sure they do theirs properly, takes over their work until one day he finds himself overloaded with other people's work, while his employees look on and criticize him.

Ibid.[15]

Philosophers often behave like little children who scribble some marks on a piece of paper at random and then ask the grown-up 'What's that?' – It happened like this: the grown-up had drawn pictures for the child several times and said: 'this is a man', 'this is a house', etc. And then the child makes some marks too and asks: what's *this* then?

Ibid.[16]

I think I summed up my attitude to philosophy when I said: philosophy ought really to be written only as a *poetic composition*.

Ibid.[17]

In philosophy the winner of the race is the one who can run most slowly. Or: the one who gets there last.

Ibid.[18]

Philosophy is a battle against the bewitchment of our intelligence by means of language.

Philosophical Investigations, 109[19]

A philosophical problem has the form: 'I don't know my way about.'

Ibid., 123[20]

Man has to awaken to wonder – and so perhaps do peoples. Science is a way of sending them to sleep again.

Miscellaneous Remarks on Culture and Value[21]

There is no more light in a genius
than in any other honest man –
but he has a particular kind of
lens to concentrate this light into
a burning point.

What is here essential for our consideration is . . . the fact that art is an adequate, metaphysics an inadequate means of the expression of the basic attitude [of a person towards life] . . . Perhaps music is the purest means of the expression of the basic attitude because it is entirely free of reference to objects. The harmonious feeling or attitude, which the metaphysician tries to express in a monistic system, is more clearly expressed in the music of Mozart. And when a metaphysician gives verbal expression to his dualistic-heroic attitude towards life in a dualistic system, is it not perhaps because he lacks the ability of a Beethoven to express this attitude in an adequate medium? **Metaphysicians are musicians without musical ability.** Instead they have a strong inclination to work within the medium of the theoretical, to connect concepts and thoughts. Now instead of activating this inclination in the domain of science and, on the other hand, satisfying the need for expression in art, the metaphysician confuses the two and produces a structure which achieves nothing for knowledge and something inadequate for the expression of attitude.

'The Elimination of Metaphysics through Logical Analysis of Language'[1]

In the strict sense . . . a sequence of words is meaningless if it does not, within a specified language, constitute a statement. It may happen that such a sequence of words looks like a statement at first glance: in that case we call it a pseudo-statement. Our thesis, now, is that logical analysis reveals the alleged statements of metaphysics to be pseudo-statements.

Ibid.[2]

To be sure, it often looks as though the word 'God' had a meaning, even in metaphysics. But the definitions which are set up prove on closer inspection to be pseudo-definitions. They lead either to logically illegitimate combinations of words . . . or to other metaphysical words (e.g. 'primordial basis', 'the absolute', 'the unconditioned', 'the autonomous', 'the self-dependent' and so forth) but in no case to the truth-conditions of its elementary sentences.

Ibid.[3]

The fact that natural languages allow the formation of meaningless sequences of words without violating the rules of grammar, indicates that grammatical syntax is, from a logical point of view, inadequate. If grammatical syntax corresponded exactly to logical syntax, pseudo-statements could not arise.

Ibid.[4]

Metaphysics. The term is used in this paper, as usually in Europe, for the field of alleged knowledge of the essence of things which transcends the realm of empirically founded, inductive science.

Ibid., Additional Note[5]

Metaphysicians are musicians without musical ability.

Whoever has emerged victorious participates to this day in the triumphal procession in which the present rulers step over those who are lying prostrate. According to traditional practice, the spoils are carried along in the procession. They are called cultural treasures, and a historical materialist 192] views them with cautious detachment. For without exception the cultural treasures he surveys have an origin which he cannot contemplate without horror. They owe their existence not only to the efforts of the great minds and talents who have created them, but also to the anonymous toil of their contemporaries. **There is no document of civilization which is not at the same time a document of barbarism.** And just as such a document is not free from barbarism, barbarism taints also the manner in which it was transmitted from one owner to another. A historical materialist therefore dissociates himself from it as far as possible. He regards it as his task to brush history against the grain.

'Theses on the Philosophy of History'[1]

Historicism contents itself with establishing a causal connection between various moments in history. But no fact that is a cause is for that very reason historical. It became historical posthumously, as it were, through events that may be separated from it by thousands of years. A historian who takes this as his point of departure stops telling the sequence of events like the beads of a rosary. Instead, he grasps the constellation which his own era has formed with a definite earlier one. Thus, he establishes a conception of the present as the 'time of the now' which is shot through with chips of Messianic time.

Ibid.[2]

Fragments of a vessel which are to be glued together must match one another in the smallest details, although they need not be like one another. In the same way a translation, instead of resembling the meaning of the original, must lovingly and in detail incorporate the original's mode of signification, thus making both the original and the translation recognizable as fragments of a greater language, just as fragments are part of a vessel. For this very reason translation must in large measure refrain from wanting to communicate something, from rendering the sense, and in this the original is important to it only insofar as it has already relieved the translator and his translation of the effort of assembling and expressing what is to be conveyed.

'The Task of the Translator'[3]

There is no document of
civilization which is not at the
same time a document of
barbarism.

At the basis of human life there exists a *principle of insufficiency*. In isolation, each man sees the majority of others as incapable or unworthy of 'being'. There is found in all free and slanderous conversation, as an animating theme, the awareness of the vanity and the emptiness of our fellow men; an apparently stagnant conversation betrays the blind and impotent flight of all life toward an indefinable summit.

The sufficiency of each being is endlessly contested by every other. Even the look that expresses love and admiration comes to me as a doubt concerning my reality.

'The Labyrinth'[1]

A man is only a particle inserted in unstable and entangled wholes.
Ibid.[2]

The world to which we have belonged offers nothing to love outside of each individual insufficiency: its existence is limited to utility. A world that cannot be loved to the point of death – in the same way that a man loves a woman – represents only self-interest and the obligation to work. If it is compared to worlds gone by, it is hideous, and appears as the most failed of all. In past worlds, it was possible to lose oneself in ecstasy, which is impossible in our world of educated vulgarity. The advantages of civilization are offset by the way men profit from them: men profit today to become the most degraded beings that have ever existed.

'The Sacred Conspiracy'[3]

It is the misunderstanding of the Earth, the forgetting of the star on which he lives, the ignorance of riches, in other words of the incandescence that is enclosed within this star, that has made for man an existence at the mercy of the merchandise he produces, the largest part of which is devoted to death. As long as men forget the true nature of terrestrial life, which demands ecstatic drunkenness and splendour, nature can only come to the attention of the accountants and economists of all parties by abandoning them to the most complete results of their accounting and economics.

'Propositions on the Death of God'[4]

At the basis of human life there
exists a *principle of insufficiency*.

A comfortable, smooth, reasonable, democratic unfreedom prevails in advanced industrial civilization, a token of technological progress. Indeed, what could be more rational than the suppression of individuality in the mechanization of socially necessary but painful performances; the concentration of individual enterprises in more effective, more productive corporations; the regulation of free competition among unequally equipped economic subjects; the curtailment of prerogatives and national sovereignties which impede the international organization of resources.

One-Dimensional Man[1]

By virtue of the way it has organized its technological base, contemporary industrial society tends to be totalitarian. For 'totalitarian' is not only a terroristic political coordination of society, but also a non-terroristic economic-technical coordination which operates through the manipulation of needs by vested interests. It thus precludes the emergence of an effective opposition against the whole. Not only a specific form of government or party-rule makes for totalitarianism, but also a specific system of production and distribution which may well be compatible with a 'pluralism' of parties, newspapers, 'countervailing powers', etc.

Ibid.[2]

In a repressive civilization, death itself becomes an instrument of repression. Whether death is feared as constant threat, or glorified as supreme sacrifice, or accepted as fate, the education for consent to death introduces an element of surrender into life from the beginning – surrender and submission. It stifles 'utopian' efforts. The powers that be have a deep affinity to death; death is a token of unfreedom, of defeat. Theology and philosophy today compete with each other in celebrating death as an existential category: perverting a biological fact into an ontological essence, they bestow transcendental blessing on the guilt of mankind which they help to perpetuate – they betray the promise of utopia.

Eros and Civilization[3]

The rejection of affluent productivity, far from being a commitment to purity, simplicity and 'nature', might be the token (and weapon) of a higher stage of human development, based on the achievements of the technological society. As the production of wasteful and destructive goods is discontinued (a stage which would mean the end of capitalism in all its forms) – the somatic and mental mutilations inflicted on man by this production may be undone. In other words, the shaping of the environment, the transformation of nature, may be propelled by the liberated rather than the repressed Life Instincts, and aggression would be subjected to their demands.

Ibid., Political Preface[4]

A comfortable, smooth,
reasonable, democratic
unfreedom prevails in advanced
industrial civilization, a token of
technological progress.

Theories are important and indispensable because without them we could not orientate ourselves in the world – we could not live. Even our observations are interpreted with their help.

'The Myth of the Framework'[1]

]

On the scientific level, the tentative adoption of a new conjecture or theory may solve one or two problems. But it invariably opens up many *new* problems, for a new, revolutionary theory functions exactly like a new and powerful sense organ. If the progress is significant then the new problems will differ from the older problems: the new problem will be on a radically different level of depth . . . This I suggest is the way in which science progresses. And our progress can best be gauged by comparing our old problems with our new ones. If the progress that has been made is great, then the new problems will be of a character undreamt-of before. There will be deeper problems and there will be more of them. The further we progress in knowledge, the more clearly we can discern the vastness of our ignorance.

'The Rationality of Scientific Revolutions'[2]

The critical tradition was founded by the adoption of the method of criticizing a received story or explanation and then proceeding to a new, improved, imaginative story which in turn is submitted to criticism. This method, I suggest, is the method of science. It seems to have been invented only once in human history. It died in the West when the schools in Athens were suppressed by a victorious and intolerant Christianity, though it lingered on in the Arab East.

'The Myth of the Framework'[3]

If the method of rational critical discussion should establish itself, then this should make the use of violence obsolete. For critical reason is the only alternative to violence so far discovered.

Ibid.[4]

In both [history and the natural sciences] we start from myths – from traditional prejudices, beset with error – and from these we proceed by criticism: by the critical elimination of errors. In both the role of evidence is, in the main, to correct our mistakes, our prejudices, our tentative theories – that is, to play a part in the critical discussion, in the elimination of error. By correcting our mistakes, we raise new problems. And in order to solve these problems, we invent conjectures, that is, tentative theories, which we submit to critical discussion, directed towards the elimination of error.

'The Philosophy of History'[5]

We could then say that rationalism is an attitude of readiness to listen to contrary arguments and to learn from experience. It is fundamentally an attitude of admitting that '*I may be wrong and you may be right and, by an effort, we may get nearer to the truth*' . . . In short, the rationalist attitude, or, as I may perhaps label it, the 'attitude of reasonableness', is very similar to the scientific attitude, to the belief that, in the search for truth, we need cooperation, and that, with the help of argument, we can in time attain something like objectivity.

The Open Society and its Enemies, 'Oracular Philosophy and the Revolt against Reason'[6]

Theories are important and
indispensable because without
them we could not orientate
ourselves in the world – we
could not live.

Philosophy, which once seemed obsolete, lives on because the moment to realize it was missed. The summary judgement that it had merely interpreted the world, that resignation in the face of reason had crippled it in itself, becomes a defeatism of reason after the attempt to change the world miscarried. Philosophy offers no place from which theory as such might be concretely convicted of the anachronisms it is suspected of, now as before. Perhaps it was an inadequate interpretation which promised that it would be put into practice. Theory cannot prolong the moment its critique depended on.

Negative Dialectics, 'The Possibility of Philosophy' [1]

Extravagant syntheses between developments in philosophy and in the natural sciences are odious, of course; they ignore the increasingly independent language of physical-mathematical formulas, a language that has long since ceased to be retrievable into visuality or any other categories directly commensurable to the consciousness of man . . . The ground of philosophical idealism, the control of nature, has lost the certainty of its omnipotence precisely because of its immense expansion during the first half of the twentieth century; also because human consciousness has limped behind, leaving the order of human affairs irrational, and finally because it took the magnitude of the attainments to let us measure their infinitesimality in comparison with the unattainable. There is a universal feeling, a universal fear, that our progress in controlling nature may increasingly help to weave the very calamity it is supposed to protect us from, that it may be weaving that second nature into which society has rankly grown.

Ibid., 'The Incapacitation of the Subject' [2]

If negative dialectics calls for the self-reflection of thinking, the tangible implication is that if thinking is to be true – if it is to be true today, in any case – it must also be a thinking against itself. If thought is not measured by the extremity that eludes the concept, it is from the outset in the nature of the musical accompaniment with which the SS liked to drown out the screams of its victims.

Ibid., 'After Auschwitz' [3]

Life in the late capitalist era is a constant initiation rite. Everyone must show that he wholly identifies himself with the power that is belabouring him.

Adorno and Max Horkheimer, *The Dialectic of Enlightenment* [4]

Philosophy, which once seemed
obsolete, lives on because the
moment to realize it was missed.

Certainly we cannot say that this man [a young student of Sartre's who in 1940 had to choose between going to England to join the Free French Forces or staying in occupied France to care for his mother, who depended on him], in choosing to remain with his mother – that is, in taking sentiment, personal devotion and concrete charity as his moral foundations – would be making an irresponsible choice, nor could we do so if he preferred the sacrifice of going away to England. **Man makes himself; he is not found ready-made; he makes himself by the choice of his morality, and he cannot but choose a morality, such is the pressure of circumstances upon him.** We define man only in relation to his commitments; it is therefore absurd to reproach us for irresponsibility in our choice.

Existentialism and Humanism[1]

Atheistic existentialism, of which I am a representative, declares with greater consistency that if God does not exist there is at least one being whose existence comes before its essence, a being which exists before it can be defined by any conception of it. That being is man . . . What do we mean by saying that existence precedes essence? We mean that man first of all exists, encounters himself, surges up in the world – and defines himself afterwards. If man as the existentialist sees him is not definable, it is because to begin with he is nothing. He will not be anything until later, and then he will be what he makes of himself. Thus, there is no human nature, because there is no God to have a conception of it. Man simply is.

Ibid.[2]

Dostoyevsky once wrote 'If God did not exist, everything would be permitted'; and that, for existentialism, is the starting point. Everything is indeed permitted if God does not exist, and man is in consequence forlorn, for he cannot find anything to depend upon either within or outside himself. He discovers forthwith that he is without excuse. For if indeed existence precedes essence, one will never be able to explain one's action by reference to a given and specified human nature: in other words, there is no determinism – man is free, man is freedom.

Ibid.[3]

I cannot make liberty my aim unless I make that of others equally my aim.

Ibid.[4]

Life is nothing until it is lived; but it is yours to make sense of, and the value of it is nothing else but the sense that you choose.

Ibid.[5]

Man makes himself; he is not found ready-made; he makes himself by the choice of his morality, and he cannot but choose a morality, such is the pressure of circumstances upon him.

The presence of the Other, a privileged heteronomy, does not clash with freedom but invests it. The shame for oneself, the presence of and desire for the other are not the negation of knowing: knowing is their very articulation. **The essence of reason consists not in securing for man a foundation and powers, but in calling him in question and in inviting him to justice.**

Totality and Infinity, 1.3, 'Truth and Justice'[1]

The Other does not affect us as what must be surmounted, enveloped, dominated, but as other, independent of us: behind every relation we could sustain with him, an absolute upsurge. It is this way of welcoming an absolute existent which we discover in justice and injustice, and which discourse, essentially teaching, effectuates.

Ibid.[2]

The transitivity of teaching, and not the interiority of reminiscence, manifests being; the locus of truth is society. The *moral* relation with the Master who judges me subtends the freedom of my adherence to the true. Thus language commences. He who speaks to me and across the words proposes himself to me retains the fundamental foreignness of the Other who judges me; our relations are never reversible.

Ibid.[3]

For the philosophical tradition of the West every relation between the same and the other, when it is no longer an affirmation of the supremacy of the same, reduces itself to an impersonal relation with a universal order. Philosophy itself is identified with the substitution of ideas for persons, the theme for the interlocutor, the interiority of the logical relation for the exteriority of interpellation. Existents are reduced to the neuter state of the idea, Being, the concept. It was to escape the arbitrariness of freedom, its disappearance into the Neuter, that we have approached the I as atheist and created . . . before the Other, who does not deliver himself in the 'thematization' or 'conceptualization' of the Other. To wish to escape dissolution into the Neuter, to posit knowing as a welcoming of the Other, is not a pious attempt to maintain the spiritualism of a personal God, but is the condition for language, without which philosophical discourse itself is but an abortive act, a pretext for an unintermitting psychoanalysis or philology or sociology, in which the appearance of discourse vanishes in the Whole.

Ibid.[4]

We do not need obscure fragments of Heraclitus to prove that being reveals itself as war to philosophical thought, that war does not only affect it as the most patent fact, but as the very patency, or the truth, of the real.

Ibid., Preface[5]

The essence of reason consists not
in securing for man a foundation
and powers, but in calling him in
question and in inviting him to
justice.

[I]f as scientists we seek simplicity, then obviously we try the simplest theory first and retreat from it only when it proves false . . . If you want to go somewhere quickly, and several alternative routes are equally likely to be open, no one asks you why you take the shortest. The simplest theory is to be chosen not because it is the most likely to be true but because it is scientifically the most rewarding among equally likely alternatives. **We aim at simplicity and hope for truth.**

'Safety, Strength, Simplicity'[1]

Rather than speak of pictures being true or false we might better speak of theories as right or wrong; for the truth of the laws of a theory is but one special feature and is often . . . overridden in importance by the cogency and compactness and comprehensiveness, the informativeness and organizing power of the whole system.

'Words, Works, Worlds'[2]

The function of a constructional system is not to recreate experience but rather to map it . . . A map is schematic, selective, condensed and uniform. And these characteristics are virtues rather than defects. The map not only summarizes, classifies and systematizes, it often discloses facts we could hardly learn immediately from our explorations . . . This also suggests the answer not only to rampant intellectualism but to many another objection against the abstraction, poverty, artificiality and general unfaithfulness of constructional systems. Let no one complain that the turnpike is not red like the line on the map, that the dotted state boundaries are not visible in the fields, or that the city we arrive at is not a round black dot. Let no one suppose that if a map made according to one scheme of projection is accurate then maps made according to alternative schemes are wrong. And let no one accuse the cartographer of reductionism if his map fails to turn green in the spring.

'The Revision of Philosophy'[3]

We are still, admittedly, in a rather primitive stage of philosophical mapmaking; and no one is to be blamed for an inclination to trust skilled verbal directions as against new and imperfect maps.

Ibid.[4]

Altogether too much philosophy is, like the present article, merely philosophy about philosophy; the characteristic refuge is not metaphysics but metaphilosophy.

Ibid.[5]

We aim at simplicity and hope for truth.

The totality of our so-called knowledge or beliefs, from the most casual matters of geography and history to the profoundest laws of atomic physics or even of pure mathematics and logic, is a man-made fabric which impinges on experience only along the edges. Or, to change the figure, total science is like a field of force whose boundary conditions are experience. A conflict with experience at the periphery occasions readjustments in the interior of the field. Truth values have to be redistributed over some of our statements. Re-evaluation of some statements entails re-evaluation of others, because of their logical interconnections – the logical laws being in turn simply further statements of the system, certain further elements of the field.

'Two Dogmas of Empiricism'[1]

As an empiricist I continue to think of the conceptual scheme of science as a tool, ultimately, for predicting future experience in the light of past experience. Physical objects are imported into the situation as convenient intermediaries – not by definition in terms of experience, but simply as irreducible posits comparable, epistemologically, to the gods of Homer. For my part I do, qua lay physicist, believe in physical objects and not in Homer's gods; and I consider it a scientific error to believe otherwise. But in point of epistemological footing the physical objects and the gods differ in degree and not in kind. Both sorts of entities enter our conception only as cultural posits. The myth of physical objects is epistemologically superior to most in that it has proved more efficacious than other myths as a device for working a manageable structure into the flux of experience.

Ibid.[2]

Each man is given a scientific heritage plus a continuing barrage of sensory stimulation; and the considerations which guide him in warping his scientific heritage to fit his continuing sensory promptings are, where rational, pragmatic.

Ibid.[3]

Language is socially inculcated and controlled; the inculcation and control turn strictly on the keying of sentences to shared stimulation. Internal factors may vary *ad libitum* without prejudice to communication as long as the keying of language to external stimuli is undisturbed. Surely one has no choice but to be an empiricist so far as one's theory of linguistic meaning is concerned.

'Epistemology Naturalized'[4]

The totality of our so-called knowledge or beliefs, from the most casual matters of geography and history to the profoundest laws of atomic physics or even of pure mathematics and logic, is a man-made fabric which impinges on experience only along the edges.

Power's condition of possibility, or in any case the viewpoint which permits one to understand its exercise, even in its more 'peripheral' effects, and which also makes it possible to use its mechanisms as a grid of intelligibility of the social order, must not be sought in the primary existence of a central point, in a unique source of sovereignty from which secondary and descendent forms would emanate; it is the moving substrate of force relations which, by virtue of their inequality, constantly engender states of power, but the latter are always local and unstable. The omnipresence of power: not because it has the privilege of consolidating everything under its invincible unity, but because it is produced from one moment to the next, at every point, or rather in every relation from one point to another. **Power is everywhere; not because it embraces everything, but because it comes from everywhere.**

The History of Sexuality, Volume 1[1]

Perhaps we should abandon the belief that power makes mad and that, by the same token, the renunciation of power is one of the conditions of knowledge. We should admit rather that power produces knowledge (and not simply by encouraging it because it serves power or by applying it because it is useful); that power and knowledge directly imply one another; that there is no power relation without the correlative constitution of a field of knowledge, nor any knowledge that does not presuppose and constitute at the same time power relations. These 'power-knowledge' relations are to be analysed, therefore, not on the basis of the subject of knowledge who is or is not free in relation to the power system, but, on the contrary, the subject who knows, the objects to be known and the modalities of knowledge must be regarded as so many effects of these fundamental implications of power-knowledge and their historical transformations.

Discipline and Punish[2]

Strangely enough, man – the study of whom is supposed by the naive to be the oldest investigation since Socrates – is probably no more than a kind of rift in the order of things, or, in any case, a configuration whose outlines are determined by the new position he has so recently taken up in the field of knowledge. Whence all the chimeras of the new humanisms, all the facile solutions of an 'anthropology' understood as a universal reflection on man, half-empirical, half-philosophical. It is comforting, however, and a source of profound relief to think that man is only a recent invention, a figure not yet two centuries old, a new wrinkle in our knowledge, and that he will disappear again as soon as that knowledge has discovered a new form.

The Order of Things, Preface[3]

The history which bears and determines us has the form of a war rather than that of a language: relations of power rather than relations of meaning. History has no 'meaning', though this is not to say that it is absurd or incoherent. On the contrary, it is intelligible and should be susceptible to analysis down to the smallest detail – but this in accordance with the intelligibility of struggles, of strategies and tactics.

'Truth and Power: An Interview'[4]

Power is everywhere; not because it embraces everything, but because it comes from everywhere.

When I claim that the murder and suffering of innocent people is wrong, I do not, I think, really care about the question whether this judgement would be valid for a being of a *totally* alien constitution and psychology. **If there are beings on, say, Alpha Centauri, who cannot feel pain and who do not mind individual death, then very likely our fuss about 'murder and suffering' will seem to them to be much ado about nothing.** But the very alienness of such a life form means that they cannot understand the moral issues involved. If our 'objectivity' is objectivity humanly speaking, it is still objectivity enough.

'Reason and History'[1]

We use our criteria of rational acceptability to build up a theoretical picture of the 'empirical world' and then as that picture develops we revise our very criteria of rational acceptability in the light of that picture and so on and so on for ever. The dependence of our methods on our picture of the world is something I have stressed in my other books; what I wish to stress here is the other side of the dependence, the dependence of the empirical world on our criteria of rational acceptability. What I am saying is that we must have criteria of rational acceptability to even have an empirical world, that these reveal part of our notion of an optimal speculative intelligence. In short, I am saying that the 'real world' depends upon our values (and, again, vice versa).

'Fact and Value'[2]

Truth cannot simply *be* rational acceptability, for one fundamental reason; truth is supposed to be a property of a statement that cannot be lost, whereas justification can be lost. The statement 'The earth is flat' was, very likely, rationally acceptable 3,000 years ago; but it is not rationally acceptable today. Yet it would be wrong to say that 'the earth is flat' was *true* 3,000 years ago; for that would mean that the earth has changed its shape. In fact rational acceptability is tensed and relative to a person. In addition rational acceptability is a matter of degree; truth is sometimes spoken of as a matter of degree (e.g. we sometimes say, *'the earth is a sphere' is approximately true*); but the 'degree' here is the *accuracy* of the statement, and not its degree of acceptability or justification.

What this shows, in my opinion, is . . . that truth is an *idealization* of rational acceptability. We speak as if there were such things as epistemically ideal conditions, and we call a statement 'true' if it would be justified under such conditions.

'Two Philosophical Perspectives'[3]

Comparison of theory with experience is *not* comparison with unconceptualized reality, even if some positivists once thought it was. It is a comparison of one or another version with the version we take to be 'experience' in the given context.

'Reflections on Goodman's *Ways of Worldmaking*'[4]

If there are beings on, say, Alpha
Centauri, who cannot feel pain
and who do not mind individual
death, then very likely our fuss
about 'murder and suffering' will
seem to them to be much ado
about nothing.

The play of differences supposes, in effect, syntheses and referrals which forbid at any moment, or in any sense, that a simple element be *present* in and of itself, referring only to itself. Whether in the order of spoken or written discourse, no element can function as a sign without referring to another element which itself is not simply present. This interweaving results in each 'element' – phonemes or graphemes – being constituted on the basis of the trace within it of the other elements of the chain or system. This interweaving, this textile, is the *text* produced only in the transformation of another text. Nothing, neither among the elements nor within the system, is anywhere ever simply present or absent. **There are only, everywhere, differences and traces of traces.**

'Semiology and Grammatology'[1]

An interval must separate the present from what it is not in order for the present to be itself, but this interval that constitutes it as present must, by the same token, divide the present in and of itself, thereby also dividing, along with the present, everything that is thought on the basis of the present, that is our metaphysical language, every being, and singularly substance or the subject. In constituting itself, in dividing itself dynamically, this interval is what might be called *spacing*, the becoming-space of time or the becoming-time of space (*temporization*). And it is this constitution of the present, as an 'originary' and irreducibly nonsimple (and, therefore, *stricto sensu* nonoriginary) synthesis of marks, or traces of retensions and protensions . . . that I propose to call archi-writing, archi-trace, or *différance*.

Which (is) (simultaneously) spacing (and) temporization.

'*Différance*'[2]

In order to exceed metaphysics it is necessary that a trace be inscribed within the text of metaphysics, a trace that continues to signal not in the direction of another presence, or another form of presence, but in the direction of an entirely other text. Such a trace cannot be thought *more metaphysico* [in a metaphysical way]. No philosopheme is prepared to master it. And it (is) that which must elude mastery. Only presence is mastered.

The mode of inscription of such a trace in the text of metaphysics is so unthinkable that it must be described as an erasure of the trace itself. The trace is produced as its own erasure. And it belongs to the trace to erase itself, to elude that which might maintain it in presence. The trace is neither perceptible nor imperceptible.

'Ousia and Gramme'[3]

All dualisms, all theories of the immortality of the soul or of the spirit, as well as all monisms, spiritualist or materialist, dialectical or vulgar, are the unique theme of a metaphysics whose entire history was compelled to strive towards the reduction of the trace. The subordination of the trace to the full presence summed up in the *logos*, the humbling of writing beneath a speech dreaming its plenitude, such are the gestures required by an onto-theology determining the archaeological and eschatological meaning of being as presence, as *parousia*, as life without *différance*: another name for death, historical metonymy where God's name holds death in check.

Of Grammatology[4]

There are only, everywhere,
differences and traces of traces.

References

Many editions and translations have been consulted in assembling this anthology. Where a translation has been used it is cited, although in some cases the wording has been altered.

ABBREVIATIONS

CDP   *Collected Dialogues of Plato*, ed. Edith Hamilton and Huntington Cairns (Princeton University Press, 1989)

CWA   *Collected Works of Aristotle*, ed. Jonathan Barnes (2 vols., Princeton University Press, 1984)

DL   Diogenes Laertius, *Lives of the Philosophers*, trans. R. D. Hicks (2 vols., Harvard University Press, 1925)

EGP   *Early Greek Philosophy*, trans. and ed. Jonathan Barnes (Penguin, 1987)

HP   *The Hellenistic Philosophers, Texts and Translations*, trans. and ed. A. A. Long and D. N. Sedley (2 vols., Cambridge University Press, 1987)

LDS   *The Last Days of Socrates: Phaedo, Socrates' Apology* and *Crito* by Plato, trans. Hugh Tredennick (Penguin, 1954)

PM   *Plutarch's Moralia*, ed. William Goodwin (5 vols., London and Cambridge, 1870)

PP   *The Presocratic Philosophers*, trans. and ed. G. S. Kirk, J. E. Raven and M. Schofield (Cambridge University Press, 1983)

U   *Utilitarianism*, ed. Mary Warnock (Fontana, 1962)

THALES

1. *EGP*, pp. 69–70.
2. Trans. W. K. C. Guthrie in Plato, *Protagoras and Meno* (Penguin, 1956); *CDP*, p. 336.

XENOPHANES

1. Xenophanes' sentences from *PP*, pp. 168–9, and my translation for the rest, based on the translation of Revd William Wilson in Clement of Alexandria, *Miscellanies* (2 vols., Edinburgh, 1867).

HERACLITUS

1. Trans. Henry Chadwick in Origen, *Contra Celsum* (Cambridge University Press, 1980).
2. My translation based on that of George Francis Legge in Saint Hippolytus of Rome, *Philosophumena or Refutation of All Heresies* (2 vols., SPCK, 1921), vol. 2, pp. 119–20.

PARMENIDES

1. *EGP*, p. 132.
2. Trans. Francis McDonald Cornford, *CDP*, p. 980.
3. *EGP*, p. 135.

ANAXAGORAS

1. *PP*, p. 394.
2. *EGP*, p. 234.
3. *PP*, p. 373.

EMPEDOCLES

1. *EGP*, p. 172.
2. My translation based on that of John Patrick, *PM*, vol. 3, p. 34.
3. *EGP*, p. 196.

PROTAGORAS

1. Trans. W. D. Ross, *CWA*, vol. 2, p. 1678.
2. Trans. Robin Waterfield (Penguin, 1987), pp. 29–30.

PHILOLAUS

1. *EGP*, pp. 221–2.
2. Ibid., pp. 203–5.
3. Trans. R. P. Hardie and R. K. Gaye, *CWA*, vol. 1, p. 346.

DEMOCRITUS

1. *EGP*, p. 270.
2. Ibid., p. 254.

PLATO

1. *LDS*, p. 107; *CDP*, p. 46.
2. *LDS*, p. 61; *CDP*, p. 15.
3. *LDS*, p. 178; *CDP*, p. 95.
4. *LDS*, pp. 71–2; *CDP*, p. 23.
5. Trans. W. D. Woodhead, *CDP*, p. 303.
6. *LDS*, p. 83; *CDP*, p. 29.
7. Trans. Walter Hamilton (Penguin, 1951), p. 83.
8. Trans. Sir Desmond Lee (Penguin, 2nd edn, 1974), p. 292.
9. Ibid., p. 263.
10. *LDS*, p. 65; *CDP*, p. 17.
11. *LDS*, pp. 135–6; *CDP*, p. 66.
12. Trans. Lee (see note 8), p. 284.
13. Trans. W. K. C. Guthrie in Plato, *Protagoras and Meno* (Penguin, 1956); *CDP*, p. 364.
14. Trans. Alexander Nehamas and Paul Woodruff (Hackett, 1995), pp. 36–7.
15. Ibid., pp. 28–9.
16. Trans. Hamilton (see note 7), p. 70.
17. Ibid., p. 94.
18. Trans. Michael Joyce, *CDP*, p. 570.

ARISTOTLE

1. Trans. W. D. Ross, *CWA*, vol. 2,
p. 1848.
2. Trans. Terence Irwin (Hackett, 1985),
pp. 265–6.
3. Ibid., pp. 286–7.
4. Trans. Ross (see note 1), vol. 2,
pp. 1554–5.
5. Ibid., p. 1555.
6. Ibid., pp. 1625–6, 1626, 1630, 1630,
1635, 1644, 1628.

EPICURUS

1. *HP*, vol. 1, p. 155.
2. Trans. and ed. Brad Inwood and
L. P. Gerson in their *Hellenistic Philosophy:
Introductory Readings* (Hackett, 1988),
p. 27.
3. Ibid., p. 26.
4. Ibid., pp. 27–8.
5. *HP*, vol. 1, p. 114.
6. Trans. Inwood and Gerson (see note
2), pp. 24–5.
7. Ibid., p. 23.

ZENO OF CITIUM

1. *HP*, vol. 1, p. 432.
2. Ibid., p. 394.
3. Ibid., p. 377.
4. Ibid., p. 382.
5. Ibid., p. 389.

ZENO'S GREEK FOLLOWERS

1. My translation, based on that of
Elizabeth Carter (London, 1758).
2. *HP*, vol. 1, p. 307.
3. Ibid., p. 381.
4. Ibid., p. 380.

5. Ibid., p. 378.
6. Ibid., p. 425.
7. Ibid., p. 192.

CICERO

1. *Cicero on the Good Life*, trans. and ed.
Michael Grant (Penguin, 1971), pp. 107–
8.
2–8. My translations from *M. Tullii
Ciceronis Opera*, ed. J. G. Baiter and C. L.
Kayser (11 vols., Leipzig, 1860–69).

LUCRETIUS

1–7. My translations from Lucretius, *De
Rerum Natura*, ed. W. H. D. Rouse
(Harvard University Press, 1924),
pp. 240, 244, 158, 230, 126, 34 and 440–
42, respectively.

PHILO OF ALEXANDRIA

1. Trans. David Winton, in Philo, *The
Contemplative Life and other Writings* (Paulist
Press, 1981), p. 15.
2. Ibid., p. 88.
3. Ibid., p. 100.
4. Ibid., p. 171.

SENECA

1. Seneca, *Letters from a Stoic*, trans. and
ed. Robin Campbell (Penguin, 1969),
p. 131.
2. My translation from *Epistulae Morales
ad Lucilium*, ed. L. D. Reynolds (2 vols.,
Clarendon, 1965), vol. 1, p. 202.
3. Trans. Campbell (see note 1), p. 130.
4. Ibid., p. 182.
5. Ibid., p. 132.

6. Ibid., p. 183.
7. Ibid., p. 198.
8. Ibid., pp. 63–4.

PLUTARCH

1. Trans. R. Kippax, *PM*, vol. 4, p. 493.
2. Ibid., p. 494.

EPICTETUS

1. Trans. Elizabeth Carter (1758), rev.
Robin Hard in Epictetus, *The Discourses
and Handbook* (Everyman, 1995),
p. 289.
2. Ibid., p. 290.
3. Ibid., p. 291.
4. Ibid., p. 306.
5. Ibid., p. 304.
6. Ibid., p. 292.

DIOGENES OF OENOANDA

1. Trans. C. W. Chilton (Oxford
University Press, 1971), p. 11.
2. Trans. John Philips, *PM*, vol. 1,
p. 481.
3. My translation from *The Annals of
Tacitus, Book 3*, ed. A. J. Woodman and
R. H. Martin (Cambridge University
Press, 1996).

SEXTUS EMPIRICUS

1. Trans. and ed. Julia Annas and
Jonathan Barnes in Sextus Empiricus,
The Outlines of Scepticism (Cambridge
University Press, 1994), p. 216.
2. Trans. and ed. Brad Inwood and
L. P. Gerson in their *Hellenistic Philosophy:
Introductory Readings* (Hackett, 1988),
p. 213.
3. Trans. Annas and Barnes (see note 1),
p. 10.
4. Ibid., pp. 10–11.

PLOTINUS

1. Trans. Thomas Taylor in Plotinus,
The Enneads (London, 1794), 6.9.
2. Ibid.
3. Ibid.
4. Ibid.
5. Ibid.

AUGUSTINE

1. Trans. R. S. Pine-Coffin (Penguin,
1961), p. 273.
2. Ibid., p. 276.
3. Ibid., p. 277.
4. Ibid., p. 278.
5. Trans. Henry Bettenson (Penguin,
1984), p. 454.

BOETHIUS

1. Trans. V. E. Watts (Penguin, 1969),
p. 79.
2. Ibid., p. 79.
3. Ibid., p. 99.

ANSELM

1. Trans. M. J. Charlesworth
(Clarendon, 1965), p. 119.
2. Ibid., p. 121.
3. Ibid., p. 135.
4. Ibid., p. 137.
5. Ibid.

BOOK OF THE TWENTY-FOUR PHILOSOPHERS

1. My translation from the French translation by Georges Poulet in his historical study *Les Métamorphoses du cercle* (Plon, 1961), p. ii. His source was *Liber XXIV Philosophorum*, ed. Clemens Baeumker in *Beträge zur Geschichte der Philosophie des Mittelalters* (1928), p. 207.
2. My translation from Poulet (see note 1), p. v. His source was Bonaventura, *Opera Omnia*, ed. Quaracchi, Collegium S. Bonaventura (10 vols., Ad Claras Aquas, 1882–1902), vol. 5, p. 91.
3. My translation from Poulet (see note 1), p. xx. His source was *Supplementum Ficinianum*, ed. Paul Oskar Kristeller (2 vols., Florence, 1937), vol. 2, p. 147.
4. My translation from Poulet (see note 1), p. xxii. His source was *Explicatio Totius Astronomiae* in Paracelsus, *Opera Omnia*, ed. Fridericus Bitiskius (3 vols., Geneva, 1658).

BONAVENTURA

1. My translation based on that of Fr Sabinus Mollitor (Heredor Book Company, 1920), pp. 34–5.
2. Trans. Ewart Cousins in Bonaventura, *The Soul's Journey unto God and other Writings* (Paulist Press, 1978), pp. 34–5.
3. My translation based on that of Fr Sabinus Mollitor (see note 1), p. 20.

AQUINAS

1. Trans. Ralph McInerny in Aquinas, *Selected Writings* (Penguin, 1998), p. 247.
2. Ibid., p. 117.
3. Ibid., p. 58.

4. Ibid., p. 561.

ECKHART

1. Trans. Oliver Davies in Eckhart, *Selected Writings* (Penguin, 1994), p. 47.
2. Ibid., p. 5.
3. Ibid., p. 41.
4. Ibid., p. 69.
5. Ibid., pp. 145–6.

WILLIAM OF OCKHAM

1. Trans. Philotheus Boehner in William of Ockham, *Philosophical Writings*, ed. Stephen F. Brown (Hackett, 1990), pp. 94–6.
2. Trans. Stephen F. Brown in ibid., p. xx, note.
3. Ibid.
4. Ibid., p. xxi.
5. Trans. Philotheus Boehner in ibid., p. 76.
6. Ibid., p. 12.
7. My translation from ibid., p. xx.

ERASMUS

1. Trans. Robert M. Adams (Norton, 1989), p. 34.
2. Ibid., p. 32.
3. Ibid., p. 54.
4. Ibid., p. 49.

MACHIAVELLI

1. Trans. George Bull (Penguin, 1961), p. 133.
2. Ibid., p. 131.

3. Trans. Leslie J. Walker, ed. Bernard
Crick (Penguin, 1971), p. 430.
4. Ibid., p. 431.

MONTAIGNE

1. Trans. M. A. Screech in Montaigne,
The Complete Essays (Penguin, 1991),
p. 623.
2. Ibid., p. 61.
3. Ibid., p. 509.
4. Ibid., p. 226.
5. Ibid., p. 514.
6. Ibid., p. 231.
7. Ibid., p. 1216.
8. Ibid., p. 1101.

VALENTIN WEIGEL

1. Trans. Steven E. Ozment in his
Mysticism and Dissent (Yale University
Press, 1973), pp. 51–2.
2. Ibid., p. 211.
3. Ibid., p. 218.
4. Ibid., p. 215.

BRUNO

1. Trans. Sidney Greenberg (King's
Crown Press, 1950), pp. 154–5.
2. *Opere Italiani*, 2.18; trans. Irving
Horowitz in his *The Renaissance Philosophy
of Giordano Bruno* (Coleman-Ross, 1952),
p. 27.
3. Trans. D. W. Singer (King's Crown
Press, 1950), p. 232.
4. Trans. Greenberg (see note 1), p. 161.
5. *Opere Italiani*, 1.316; trans. Horowitz
(see note 2), p. 60.

FRANCIS BACON

1. Trans. R. Ellis and James Spedding in
Bacon, *The Works of Francis Bacon* (2 vols.,
Routledge, 1905), vol. 1, p. 66.
2. Ibid., p. 68.
3. Ibid., p. 77.
4. Ibid., p. 148.
5. *Essays*, ed. Michael J. Hawkins
(Everyman, 1994), p. 42.
6. Ibid., p. 129.

HOBBES

1. Ed. C. B. Macpherson (Penguin,
1985), p. 106. (Spelling modernized.)
2. Ibid., pp. 111–12.
3. *The Elements of Law, Natural and Politic*,
ed. F. Tonnies (Cambridge University
Press, 1928), p. 6.
4. Ibid., p. 22.
5. Ibid., p. 150.
6. Ed. Macpherson (see note 1),
p. 185.
7. Ibid., pp. 189–90.

DESCARTES

1. Trans. E. S. Haldane and G. R. T.
Ross (Encyclopaedia Britannica, Great
Books of the Western World, 1954),
p. 3.
2. Ibid., p. 7.
3. Trans. Desmond Clarke in Descartes,
Meditations and other Metaphysical Writings
(Penguin, 1998), pp. 55–6.
4. Trans. Haldane and Ross (see note 1),
p. 283.

LA ROCHEFOUCAULD

1. Trans. Leonard Tancock (Penguin, 1959), p. 38.
2. Ibid., p. 38.
3. Ibid., p. 55.
4. Ibid., p. 65.
5. Ibid., p. 72.
6. Ibid., p. 115.
7. Ibid., pp. 41–2.
8. Ibid., p. 46.
9. Ibid., p. 47.

PASCAL

1. Trans. A. J. Krailsheimer (Penguin, 1966), p. 59.
2. Ibid., pp. 67–8.
3. Ibid., p. 48.
4. Ibid., p. 38.
5. Ibid., p. 59.
6. Ibid., p. 72.

ANGELUS SILESIUS

1–6. The quotations are revised versions of the translations made by Mary Shady in Angelus Silesius, *The Cherubinic Wanderer: A Selection* (Paulist Press, 1986).

SPINOZA

1. Trans. Edwin Curley (Penguin, 1996), p. 62.
2. Ibid., p. 69.
3. Ibid., p. 72.
4. Ibid., p. 73.

JOHN LOCKE

1. *An Essay Concerning Human Understanding: An Abridgment*, ed. John Yolton (Dent, 1977), pp. 39–40.
2. Ibid., p. 76.
3. Ibid., p. 248.

LEIBNIZ

1. Trans. Roger Ariew and Daniel Garber in Leibniz, *Philosophical Essays* (Hackett, 1989), p. 210.
2. Ibid., p. 211.
3. Ibid., p. 221.

VICO

1. Trans. Thomas Goddard Bergin and Max Harold Fisch (Cornell University Press, 1984), pp. 265–6.
2. Ibid., p. 67.
3. Ibid., p. 63.
4. Ibid., p. 120.

BERKELEY

1. Ed. R. M. Adams (Hackett, 1979), p. 44.
2. Berkeley, *Philosophical Works*, ed. Michael R. Ayers (Everyman, 1993), p. 91.
3. Ed. Adams (see note 1), p. 30.

MONTESQUIEU

1. Trans. Thomas Nugent (2 vols., London, 1878), vol. 1, p. 6.
2. Ibid., p. 7.
3. Ibid., p. 50.

VOLTAIRE

1. Trans. Theodore Besterman (Penguin, 1971), p. 391.
2. Ibid., p. 389.
3. Ibid., p. 392.
4. Ibid., p. 275.
5. Ibid., p. 182.
6. Ibid., p. 274.
7. Ibid., p. 270.

LA METTRIE

1. Trans. Ann Thompson in La Mettrie, *Machine Man and other Writings* (Cambridge University Press, 1996), pp. 15, 17.
2. Ibid., p. 68.
3. Ibid., p. 24.
4. Ibid., p. 15.
5. Ibid., p. 38.

HUME

1. *Essays: Literary, Political and Moral* (Oxford University Press, 1963), p. 593.
2. Ibid., p. 590.
3. Ibid., p. 591.
4. Ibid., p. 604.
5. Ed. L. A. Selby-Bigge (Clarendon, 1978), p. 259.
6. Ibid., p. 262.
7. Ibid., p. 654.
8. Ibid., p. 139.
9. Ibid., p. 247.

ROUSSEAU

1. Trans. G. D. H. Cole in Rousseau, *The Social Contract and Discourses* (Dent, 1968), p. 3.
2. My translation from *Œuvres complètes*, ed. Bernard Gagnebin and Marcel Raymond (4 vols., Éditions de la Pléiade, 1964), vol. 3, p. 491.
3. Ibid., p. 841.
4. Ibid., p. 481.
5. Trans. Cole (see note 1), p. 211.
6. My translation from *Œuvres complètes* (see note 2), vol. 4, p. 524n.
7. Ibid., vol. 3, p. 498.

DIDEROT

1. Trans. Michael Henry (Penguin, 1986), p. 21.
2-7. My translations from *Œuvres complètes*, ed. Laurent Versini (2 vols., Laffort, 1994), vol. 1, pp. 27, 29, 44, 45, 1137 and 1137, respectively.

CONDILLAC

1. Trans. Franklin Philip and Harlan Lane in Condillac, *Philosophical Writings* (Lawrence Erblaum, 1982), p. 11.
2. Ibid., p. 123.
3. Ibid., p. 337.

KANT

1. Trans. Norman Kemp Smith (St Martin's Press, 1965), p. 93.
2. Ibid., p. 82.
3. Ibid., p. 126.
4. Trans. H. J. Paton (Harper, 1964), pp. 95-6.
5. Ibid., p. 84.
6. Ibid., p. 88.
7. Trans. Lewis White Beck in Kant, *On History* (Macmillan, 1963), p. 21.
8. Trans. Lewis White Beck (University of Chicago Press, 1949), p. 258.

9. Trans. J. H. Bernard (Macmillan, 1914), p. 188.
10. Trans. Werner S. Pluhar (Hackett, 1987), p. 175.
11. Ibid., p. 177.
12. Trans. Bernard (see note 9), p. 215.
13. Trans. Beck in Kant, *On History* (see note 7), p. 3.
14. Ibid., p. 12.
15. Ibid., p. 16.
16. Ibid., pp. 22–3.
17. Ibid., p. 116.

LICHTENBERG

1. Trans. Franz Mautner and Harry Hatfield (Jonathan Cape, 1969), p. 44.
2. Ibid., p. 58.
3. Ibid., p. 30.
4. Ibid., p. 31.
5. Ibid., p. 59.
6. Ibid., p. 61.
7. Ibid., p. 62.
8. Ibid., p. 40.

BENTHAM

1. *Collected Works*, ed. J. H. Burns (8 vols., Athlone Press, 1968–), vol. 4, p. 316.
2. H. L. A. Hart (Athlone Press, 1970), p. 2.
3. *Economic Writings*, ed. W. Stark (3 vols., Allen & Unwin for the Royal Economic Society, 1952), vol. 1, p. 82.
4. *U*, p. 34.
5. (3 vols., Alcan, 1901–4), vol. 1, p. 412.

FICHTE

1. Trans. Peter Heath and John Lachs (Appleton-Century-Crofts, 1970), p. 6.
2. Ibid., p. 38.
3. Ibid., p. 246.

SCHLEIERMACHER

[**225**

1. Trans. Horace Leland Friess (Open Court, 1926), p. 60.
2. Ibid., pp. 51–2.
3. Ibid., p. 56.
4. Trans. John W. Oman (Kegan Paul, 1893), pp. 49–50.

HEGEL

1. Trans. A. V. Miller (Oxford University Press, 1977), p. 27.
2. Ibid., p. 11.
3. Trans. T. M. Knox (Oxford University Press, 1967), p. 10.
4. Trans. Miller (see note 1), p. 43.
5. Ibid., p. 114.
6. Ibid., p. 111.
7. Trans. Knox (see note 3), pp. 23–4.

SCHLEGEL

1. Trans. Peter Firchow in Schlegel, *Lucinde and the Fragments* (University of Minnesota Press, 1971), p. 189.
2. Ibid., p. 164.
3. Ibid., p. 199.
4. Ibid., p. 215.
5. Ibid., p. 248.
6. Ibid., p. 250.
7. Ibid., p. 230.
8. Ibid., p. 243.
9. Ibid.
10. Ibid., p. 251.

11. Ibid., pp. 176–7.
12. Trans. James Burton Robinson
(London, 6th edn, 1848), p. 66.

CLAUSEWITZ

1. Trans. Col. J. J. Graham, rev. Col.
F. N. Maude, ed. Anatol Rapoport
(Penguin, 1982), pp. 116–17.
2. Ibid., p. 101.
3. Ibid., p. 102.
4. Ibid., p. 119.

SCHOPENHAUER

1. Trans. R. J. Hollingdale in
Schopenhauer, *Essays and Aphorisms*
(Penguin, 1970), p. 51.
2. Trans. E. F. J. Payne (2 vols., Dover,
1969), vol. 1, p. 280.
3. Ibid., p. 281.
4. Ibid.
5. Trans. Hollingdale (see note 1), p. 42.

COMTE

1. Trans. Harriet Martineau in *Auguste
Comte and Positivism*, ed. Gertrud Lenzer
(University of Chicago Press, 1975),
p. 73.
2. Ibid., p. 73.
3. Ibid., p. 82.
4. Ibid., p. 381.

MILL

1. *U*, pp. 196–7.
2. Ibid., p. 130.
3. Ibid., p. 135.
4. Ibid., p. 159.
5. Ibid., p. 143.

PROUDHON

1. Trans. John Beverly Robinson
(Freedom Press, 1923), pp. 293–4.
2. Trans. Benjamin Tucker (2 vols.,
New York, 1898), vol. 1, p. 37.
3. Ibid., p. 41.

KIERKEGAARD

1. Trans. Alaister Hannay (Penguin,
1992), p. 482.
2. Ibid., p. 491.
3. Trans. Harold Hong and Edna Hong
(Princeton University Press, 1992),
p. 257.
4. Trans. Harold Hong and Edna Hong
(Princeton University Press, 1990), p. 335.
5. Ibid., p. 370.
6. Trans. Alaister Hannay (Penguin,
1989), p. 48.
7. Ibid., p. 57.
8. Ibid., p. 95.
9. Ibid., p. 89.

MARX AND ENGELS

1. Trans. R. Pascal in Marx, *The Portable
Marx*, ed. Eugene Kamenka (Penguin,
1983), p. 170.
2. Ibid., pp. 177–9.
3. Ibid., p. 203.
4. Ibid., p. 222.

NIETZSCHE

1. Trans. Walter Kaufmann (Vintage,
1974), p. 233.
2. Trans. Walter Kaufmann in
Nietzsche, *The Birth of Tragedy and
The Case of Wagner* (Vintage, 1967),
p. 141.

3. Trans. Kaufmann (see note 1),
p. 163.

4. Trans. Walter Kaufmann (Vintage,
1966), p. 87.

5. Trans Kaufmann (see note 1),
p. 181.

6. Trans. Walter Kaufmann in
Nietzsche, *The Genealogy of Morals and
Ecce Homo* (Vintage, 1967), p. 90.

7. Trans. Kaufmann (see note 4),
p. 71.

8. Trans. Walter Kaufmann and R. J.
Hollingdale (Vintage, 1968), p. 35.

9. Trans. R. J. Hollingdale (Penguin,
1968), pp. 40–41.

10. Trans. Kaufmann and Hollingdale
(see note 8), pp. 549–50.

11. Trans. R. J. Hollingdale (Penguin,
1969), p. 46.

POINCARÉ

1. Trans. 'W.J.G.' (Walter Scott
Publishing Co., 1905), p. 140.

2. Ibid., p. 141.

3. Ibid., p. 143.

4. Ibid.

5. Ibid., p. 144.

6. Ibid., p. 159.

HUSSERL

1. Trans. W. R. Boyce Gibson (Allen &
Unwin, 1931), p. 153.

2. Ibid., p. 154.

3. Ibid., p. 111.

4. Trans. Dorion Cairns in Husserl,
Cartesian Meditations (Kluwer, 1991),
p. 91.

DEWEY

1. *John Dewey: The Essential Writings*, ed.
David Sidorsky (Harper, 1977), pp. 6–7.

2. Ibid., p. 7.

3. Ibid., p. 229.

McTAGGART

1. (Cambridge University Press, 1921),
pp. 11–12.

2. Ibid., p. 13.

3. Ibid., p. 19.

4. Ibid., p. 22.

RUSSELL

1. *Why I am not a Christian* (Allen &
Unwin, 1957), p. 48.

2. Ibid., p. 62.

3. Ibid., pp. 61–2.

4. (Allen & Unwin, 1961), p. 789.

NEURATH

1. Trans. George Schlick in *Logical
Positivism*, ed. A. J. Ayer (Free Press,
1966), p. 201.

2. Ibid., p. 200.

JASPERS

1. Trans. R. F. C. Hall and Grete Wels
(Harcourt, Brace, 1968), p. 8.

2. Ibid., p. 10.

3. Ibid., p. 11.

4. Ibid., p. 26.

5. Ibid., p. 35.

6. Ibid., pp. 111–12.

7. Ibid., p. 116.

HEIDEGGER

1. Trans. Frank A. Capuzzi with J. Glenn Gray and David Farrell Krell in *Heidegger: Basic Writings*, ed. D. Farrell Krell (Harper, 1977), p. 193.
2. Ibid., p. 206.
3. Ibid., p. 211.
4. Ibid., p. 219.
5. Trans. Peter D. Hertz in Heidegger, *On the Way to Language* (Harper, 1971), pp. 26–7.
6. Trans. Albert Hofstadter in Heidegger, *Poetry, Language, Thought* (Harper, 1971), p. 210.

WITTGENSTEIN

1. Trans. G. H. Von Wright (Blackwell, 1980), p. 18e.
2. Trans. C. K. Ogden (Routledge & Kegan Paul, 1981), pp. 149–51.
3. Ibid., p. 65.
4. Ibid., p. 79.
5. Ibid.
6. Ibid., p. 189.
7. Trans. Wright (see note 1), p. 57e.
8. Trans. G. E. M. Anscombe (Blackwell, 1968), p. 146e.
9. Ibid., pp. 44–5e.
10. Ibid., p. 11e.
11. Ibid., p. 47e.
12. Trans. Wright (see note 1), p. 35e.
13. Ibid.
14. Ibid., p. 16e.
15. Ibid.
16. Ibid., p. 17e.
17. Ibid., p. 24e.
18. Ibid., p. 34e.
19. Trans. Anscombe (see note 8), p. 47e.
20. Ibid., p. 49e.
21. Trans. Wright (see note 1), p. 5e.

CARNAP

1. Trans. Arthur Pap in *Logical Positivism at its Peak*, ed. S. Sarker (Garland Publishing, 1996), p. 30.
2. Ibid., p. 11.
3. Ibid., p. 16.
4. Ibid., p. 18.
5. Ibid., p. 26.

BENJAMIN

1. Trans. Harry Zohn in Benjamin, *Illuminations*, ed. Hannah Arendt (Schocken, 1969), pp. 256–7.
2. Ibid., p. 263.
3. Ibid., p. 78.

BATAILLE

1. Trans. Allan Stoekl in Bataille, *Visions of Excess 1927–1939* (University of Minnesota Press, 1985), p. 172.
2. Ibid., p. 174.
3. Ibid., p. 179.
4. Ibid., p. 201.

MARCUSE

1. (Ark, 1986), p. 1.
2. Ibid., p. 3.
3. (Beacon Press, 1966), p. 236.
4. Ibid., p. xix.

POPPER

1. Popper, *The Myth of the Framework*, ed. M. A. Notturno (Routledge, 1994), p. 53.
2. Ibid., p. 4.
3. Ibid., p. 38.
4. Ibid., p. 69.

5. Ibid., p. 141.
6. (2 vols., Routledge & Kegan Paul, 1962), vol. 2, p. 225.

ADORNO

1. Trans. E. B. Ashton (Continuum, 1973), p. 3.
2. Ibid., p. 67.
3. Ibid., p. 365.
4. Trans. John Cumming (Verso, 1989), p. 153.

SARTRE

1. Trans. Philip Mairet (Methuen, 1973), p. 50.
2. Ibid., p. 28.
3. Ibid., p. 34.
4. Ibid., p. 52.
5. Ibid., p. 54.

LEVINAS

1. Trans. Alphonso Lingis (Duquesne University Press, 1969), p. 88.
2. Ibid., p. 89.
3. Ibid., p. 101.
4. Ibid., pp. 87–8.
5. Ibid., p. 22.

GOODMAN

1. *Problems and Projects* (Bobbs-Merrill, 1972), p. 352.
2. *Ways of Worldmaking* (Hackett, 1978), p. 19.
3. *Problems and Projects* (see note 1), p. 15.
4. Ibid., p. 17.
5. Ibid., pp. 21–2.

QUINE

1. *From a Logical Point of View* (Harvard University Press, 1953), p. 42.
2. Ibid., p. 44.
3. Ibid., p. 46.
4. *Ontological Relativity and other Essays* (Harvard University Press, 1969), p. 81.

FOUCAULT

1. Trans. Robert Hurley (3 vols., Penguin, 1984), vol. 1, p. 93.
2. Trans. Alan Sheridan (Penguin, 1979), p. 28.
3. Trans. Alan Sheridan (Tavistock/Routledge, 1989), p. xxiii.
4. Trans. Colin Gordon in *The Foucault Reader*, ed. Paul Rabinow (Penguin, 1984), p. 56.

PUTNAM

1. *Reason, Truth and History* (Cambridge University Press, 1981), p. 168.
2. Ibid., p. 135.
3. Ibid., p. 55.
4. *Reason and Realism: Philosophical Papers Vol. 3* (Cambridge University Press, 1983), p. 162.

DERRIDA

1. Trans. Alan Bass in Derrida, *Positions* (University of Chicago Press, 1981), p. 26.
2. Trans. Alan Bass in Derrida, *Margins of Philosophy* (University of Chicago Press, 1986), p. 13.
3. Ibid., p. 65.
4. Trans. Gayatri Chakravorty Spivak (Johns Hopkins University Press, 1976), p. 71.